From a Victorian Garden

From a Victorian Garden

CREATING THE ROMANCE OF A BYGONE AGE

RIGHT IN YOUR OWN BACKYARD

Michael Weishan

- AND -

Cristina Roig

Color photography by Susan Seubert

[Viking Studio}

VIKING STUDIO
Published by the Penguin Group
Penguin Group (USA) Inc., 375 Hudson Street, New York, New York 10014, U.S.A.
Penguin Books Ltd, 80 Strand, London WC2R 0RL, England
Penguin Books Australia Ltd, 250 Camberwell Road, Camberwell, Victoria 3124, Australia
Penguin Books Canada Ltd, 10 Alcorn Avenue, Toronto, Ontario, Canada M4V 3B2
Penguin Books India (P) Ltd, 11 Community Centre, Panchsheel Park, New Delhi – 110 017, India
Penguin Books (N.Z.) Ltd, Cnr Rosedale and Airborne Roads, Albany, Auckland, New Zealand
Penguin Books (South Africa) (Pty) Ltd, 24 Sturdee Avenue, Rosebank, Johannesburg 2196, South Africa

Penguin Books Ltd, Registered Offices: 80 Strand, London WC2R 0RL, England

First published in 2004 by Viking Studio, a member of Penguin Group (USA) Inc.

1 3 5 7 9 10 8 6 4 2

Copyright © Michael Weishan and Cristina Roig, 2004
Photographs copyright © Susan Seubert, 2004
All rights reserved

CIP data available

ISBN 0-670-89426-5

Printed in Korea
Set in ITC Century Light and Century Expanded

DESIGNED BY JAYE ZIMET

To Cynthia and Laurie

Sorores optimaeque maximae

PREFACE

Not too long ago a friend asked me how *From a Victorian Garden* got started. I chuckled to myself for while the process of literary creation is normally quite straightforward, at least for me, the path to creating *this* particular book was anything but. In fact, I would go so far to say that it required a concerted act of the gods to will this book into creation—its genesis was due to a series of totally random events; its generation much harder and more complicated than I would have ever imagined; and its completion only achieved, in retrospect at least, through seemingly divine intervention.

It all started innocently enough. In the fall of 1998, my mother and I decided to take a trip to the Pacific Northwest. Neither Mom nor I had ever been there, and although I was very busy at the time finishing up the proofs of my first book, *The New Traditional Garden*, I thought that it would be a great idea to familiarize myself with the gardens in that part of the world before it went to press. So I cleared some time in my schedule, and

off we went. It was a wonderful trip. My mother proved to be the perfect companion, an enthusiastic garden tourist, cheerfully tramping her way through dozens of lovely, albeit soggy, gardens in Portland, Seattle, and then finally up into British Columbia.

We arrived in Vancouver with the basic intention of remaining in the city and limiting ourselves to horticultural sites in the immediate area, of which there are many. But I kept hearing wonderful tales of the gardens of Victoria, the capital of British Columbia, which as the crow flies is only about forty miles away. Unfortunately, crows can fly over water, and that's what it takes to get to Victoria. (How Victoria, an island inaccessible by bridge or tunnel, surrounded by stormy, fog-bound seas, wound up becoming the provincial capital, and holding on to that honor, is a long, fascinating story, which unfortunately we don't have the time to tell here.) For our purposes, the critical factor was that Victoria, with its tantalizing gardens, lay glimmering on the Western horizon just visible from the windows of our hotel room, across the Georgia straits.

We did a little investigating and found out that though it is *possible* to get to Victoria and back in one day without spending a fortune to fly by heli-jet, it's not pleasant. It requires a five o'clock wake-up, an hour drive to the ferry terminal, a several-hour ferry ride, and another half-hour drive into Victoria proper. And that's just one way. Spending an additional day there was out of the question since I was due back on the East Coast in two days, and neither Mom nor I was very sure that we wanted to endure rigors of that kind for gardens we didn't know much about at the tail end of a long trip. And there was yet another consideration: Anyone who knows me knows that after extremely early wake-ups, my next least favorite thing in the world is sea travel; my mother, remembering our last *mal de mer* ferry crossing of the English Channel, wasn't too excited by the idea either. Prospects of seeing Victoria were dimming by the minute. Then the first twist of fate occurred.

Through pure chance and the good offices of Vancouver's Board of Tourism, which had arranged our accommodations, I had been introduced to Stephen Darling, who was manager of our hotel, the Westin Grand. Stephen, who as it turned out was a great gardener himself, suggested that we should in fact make the effort to get to Victoria, as it was well worth it. Trying to narrow down our itinerary to a manageable day plan, I asked him about the various gardens mentioned in our guide, including an obscure one called Point Ellice House. Knowing a bit about the book I was writing and my interest in history, he assured me

that this garden was well worth seeing. His enthusiastic report provided the impetus we required.

So the next morning, or should I say night, as it was pitch black at 5:00 A.M., Mom and I awoke to the sound of pouring rain. Lying there in my warm bed, snug under a delightful down comforter, I quickly decided that this plan wasn't one of my most well considered, and I told my mother so in my best predawn tone when she tried to roust me. There was just no way, no way in bloody blazes, that I was going out in the total darkness in this kind of weather. Inured to my complaints through years of experience, she would hear none of it. "I know you, Michael," she said, "and I know full well that if we don't go we'll never hear the end of it, constantly moaning about those gardens we didn't see because you were too lazy. So get out of bed!" Fate, in the person of maternal sagacity, had intervened again.

After a long bathroom-less ride and an excruciating wait in the ferry line, in which we both regretted all the coffee we had consumed, we finally got on board, and ultimately reached the island. We saw several gardens there, including the famed Buchart Gardens, which my mother truly enjoyed, but which really weren't my cup of tea. For me at least, the day so far had been long, wet, cold, and not particularly rewarding. We had time to see just one more garden, Point Ellice, which our guidebook said was located in downtown Victoria. With my mother as map reader, off we set.

A frustrating hour and a half later we were completely lost in what looked to be some industrial area of the city, and the normal bonhomie between my favorite navigator and myself began to fray. The tour book clearly said that the house was located on Pleasant Street. We *seemed* to be on Pleasant Street, yet all we could see were huge piles of rocks and scrap metal. "This *can't* be right, Mother," I said through gritted teeth. "I don't know what to tell you," she replied. "According to the map, we've arrived. Why not just go down to the end of the street and turn around? Then we can go find someone to ask." Wise maternal advice. I continued down the road in preparation to turn around, and there near the end, my eye caught a glimpse of green. In the midst of this wasteland, there sat two verdant acres surrounding what appeared to be a gemlike Victorian house.

Despite my surprise at the surrounding area, something told me that this wasn't your average tourist site, and I couldn't wait to get inside. We pulled into the parking lot, got out of the car, headed for the gate, and stopped dead. "Closed for the season," the sign read. Gloom, doom, and destruction! This was really the last straw! Getting up at five, hours in the car and on the sea, the prospect of more of the same to get back to Vancouver, and the one garden that really looked intriguing was closed. I, for the lack of a better word, proceeded to have a small tantrum in front of the locked gate, bewailing my fate to the heavens in a very loud voice, with my mother, who abhors scenes, ostensibly attempting to console me, but secretly wondering if I hadn't grown up at all in the last thirty-five years. Suddenly, a face appeared behind the gate. The gods to the rescue again.

"May I help you?" the face asked, in that wonderfully clipped, half-British accent so typical of Victoria. "I heard the noise from inside and wondered if something weren't wrong." With a sudden and half-successful attempt to regain my composure, I said: "I'm Michael Weishan, and this is my mom. I'm working on a book on historic gardens, and I very much wanted to see the house and garden, but I see you are closed for the season, etc., etc., etc. Our guidebook neglected to tell us that fact, etc., etc., etc., *and we've come all the way from Boston!*" This last I practically wailed. To my surprise and pleasure, the face replied, "Well, by all means come on in, I only have a half hour or so, but I would be happy to show you around. Let's start with the house."

And thus, gentle reader, was born the book that you hold in your hands for what I saw inside that house and grounds was absolutely extraordinary: a perfectly preserved Victorian homestead, which had remained in the same family for over a hundred years, *complete with its contents.* This last fact was the key. While it's not unusual to find a historic structure preserved, normally the contents have been scattered to the four winds. Occasionally, you may come upon a site with some original furnishings. But it's absolutely unheard of to find a house filled to the rafters with the possessions of the original owners, looking almost exactly as they left them.

Walking into Point Ellice House was like stepping back in time. Nothing had changed in one hundred years. As I toured room after room, replete with all the bric-a-brac of Victorian life, my guide told the story of the family that had lived here, the O'Reillys, and how they had saved *everything.* "Everything," I asked? "Everything, not just their furniture, but also their books, letters to each other over forty years, magazines, pictures, clothes, even seed catalogues with their selections marked in them."

My mouth dropped as we passed outside to the grounds. Walking across the perfectly flat croquet lawn past 120-year-old hollies, beds of ancient roses, and gently trailing ivy, I was told that the landscape had been partially restored according to the plans, plant lists, and correspondence of the owners, all of which had been preserved. Through careful rejuvenation, many of the plants themselves dated from the Victorian age. I could hardly believe it. Not only was the house intact, but the contents, and the letters, and the plans, even pictures of the grounds remained as well. This was a veritable treasure trove. "Of course it's been published. . . ." I asked, awaiting the near inevitable disappointment. "Not to my knowledge," came back the reply. I had entered an author's nirvana.

While my mother toured more of the house, which included a lesson on the Point Ellice House ghosts (the house is supposedly quite haunted, but that I can neither aver nor deny, gratefully having been spared any supernatural occurrences), I tried to assemble as much information as I could to take back with me. Some pictures, basic history, brochures, phone numbers of people in charge, anything that could help me pull together my ideas for I was beginning to think that this would make a great gardening book. Gathering up an armload of documentation, we headed for the car. The last ferry of the day was approaching fast, and with some very heartfelt thanks to our tour guide, Mom and I returned to Vancouver.

Back in Boston, I immediately contacted a colleague, Cristina Roig Morris, and explained to her my idea for the book. Given the size and complexity of the project, and her experience with color photography (for unlike *The New Traditional Garden*, which was done with all black-and-white period images, I was thinking that this book would be full of color), I asked her if she would be interested in working on the project, and she immediately agreed. We set about preparing a proposal, and ultimately through the offices of our agent, Colleen Moyhyde, the book went to Viking. A very talented, up-and-coming photographer, Susan Seubert, was then hired to handle the color photography. The team in place, we began to work. Almost immediately, problems occurred. Scheduling photo shoots proved exceedingly difficult in the fickle weather of Victoria. Roses opened and closed in a day, awnings would suddenly detach from the house in the wind, even aphids interfered. Who wants to see a close-up shot of a flower covered with bugs? The Point Ellice grounds are gardened organically, a highly commendable undertaking, but the occasional insects that inevitably arise are a photographer's nightmare.

To make matters worse, the very thing that had initially appeared to be our salvation, the thousands of pages of records and documents the O'Reilly family had saved, almost proved to be our undoing. There was *so much* material to review that additional trips back and forth across the continent had to be scheduled, immediately and substantially overrunning a very tight budget. Fortunately, through the kind offices of the Canadian Heritage Branch in the persons of curators John Adams, Jennifer Iredale, and curatorial assistant Theresa Molinaro, we were able to whittle down the mass of documents and photos to an almost manageable amount. At last, it seemed, the book was well under way with nothing but clear sailing ahead; I soon discovered, however, it's always unwise for mere mortals to presume too much.

The reward for my overconfidence was a sudden, major blow: My colleague Cristina announced a gardening project of her own, the imminent birth of her son Luke Anthony, which, while a joyous event in itself, in essence meant her withdrawal from the book only months before the publisher's deadline. And at Viking, the initial editor who had guided our project from the beginning unexpectedly announced *she too* was leaving to have a baby. Some very anxious weeks ensued, but fate once again was kind. Cristina's mantle was ably assumed by our good friend and colleague George Homsy, who completed and expanded Cristina's initial drafts, while our new editor, Elissa Altman, proved to be a fine replacement as well. Thus, six years, innumerable plot twists, character changes, and many, many thousands of miles later, you now have before you the result of our efforts.

If we have done our job correctly, you'll find that we have produced not just a historical volume documenting this truly remarkable house, garden, and family, but also a modern, practical guide to allow today's homeowners to re-create the beauty of a Victorian-era garden right in their own backyards. Of course, it's easy to be blinded by the ro-

mance of a bygone age, and we fully acknowledge that there are many aspects of the Victorian era and culture that are not practical, or even desirable, to replicate in the twenty-first century. But in terms of the landscape at least, the period that created the Point Ellice House gardens represents one of the acmes of Western horticulture, revealing many invaluable lessons that we would be wise to keep in mind today—from simple things like planting historic annuals, to larger projects like creating your own woodland garden. Even the scale of the Point Ellice grounds lends itself to this process. The modest two and a half acres, so similar to many of today's lots, show how successfully one can blend landscape and architecture in a small space to produce a wonderfully integrated house and garden, a quality sorely lacking in modern landscapes. So whether you are interested in a model for a new period landscape, or want to add a touch of romance to an existing garden, or simply are fascinated by the glories of a long lost era, the following pages hold something for you. Enjoy!

Michael Weishan
Boston
March 2004

ACKNOWLEDGMENTS

With any book of this size and scope, the number of individuals and institutions involved is huge, and a complete list of acknowledgments could go on for ages. However, there are certain people, who, by their extraordinary effort and determination, helped to bring this manuscript to publication. To these I owe special thanks:

First and foremost, to the stellar trio at B.C. Heritage—John Adams, Jennifer Iredale, and Theresa Molinaro—who so generously gave their time, experience, and knowledge and without whom, to put new meaning to the old phrase, this book couldn't have been even contemplated. They and the entire Point Ellice curatorial and archaeological staff, as well as that at the B.C. Archives—especially Julie Warren—were instrumental in every phase of this project.

To Stephen Darling, manager of the Westin Grand in Vancouver, who was the one to suggest I go to Point Ellice in the first place and who never failed to provide a warm and hospitable welcome throughout many years of visits.

To my mother, Carol Weishan, who never flagged in her enthusiasm for visiting gardens in all weathers, climates, and conditions, and who never lost patience with her sometimes-trying son.

To Nancy Soriano and Marjorie Gage, my editors and friends at *Country Living Magazine*, who kindly gave their permission to expand and adapt a number of topics that originally had their genesis in my monthly column, "Your Garden."

To our photographer, Susan Seubert, whose cheery countenance and professionalism, not to mention her extraordinary photo talents, truly brought this project to life.

To Christopher Spence, my editorial assistant, who labored tirelessly over text and drawings, not to mention keeping my office functioning, garden watered, and dogs fed during my many long absences.

To Cristina Roig Morris, my college chum, companion of twenty years, and former business partner, who showed me the exact value of our friendship.

To George Homsy, the unsung hero of this manuscript, who held everything together when all seemed to be falling apart.

And finally, to my literary agent, Colleen Mohyde, who endured more than anyone ever should helping to birth a single book.

Again my thanks to each and every one of you, and to everyone else who helped to create *From a Victorian Garden.*

Michael Weishan
Boston, March 2004

CONTENTS

CHAPTER VIII
HOW SCIENCE CAME TO THE GARDEN
-OR-
HOW WE KNOW WHAT WE KNOW
ABOUT THE POINT ELLICE LANDSCAPE
87

EPILOGUE
97

APPENDIX
PERIOD PROJECTS, PARTICULARS,
AND PECULIARITIES
105

INTRODUCTION
THE O'REILLYS AND POINT ELLICE HOUSE

A Garden Revealed • The Setting, Cast, and Characters • Why We Garden • Gardeners Nearly Lost at Sea

A Garden Revealed

It's very hard, when peering into a musty old print, to appreciate the true essence of the Victorian garden. The pictures are, of course, wonderfully quaint and charming. But often these images by themselves allow us no real entry into the garden. To the twenty-first-century viewer, accustomed to three-dimensional thinking in dynamic color, these pictures have become just too remote. Their very black-and-whiteness betrays the fact that the world has changed too much. The people who dreamed these gardens into reality have long returned to dust, the mores and customs that drove their creation are by now so strange as to be almost foreign, and in many cases, the very places and plants have long since disappeared.

Yet despite these handicaps and across all these years, something about these gardens still manages to call to us. If only we could just enter and find out what! The Victorian garden seems so *comforting*—solid and self-assured in a way our land-scapes today completely lack. You may not admire every element of Victorian taste, nor would you want to duplicate this or that in your own land-scape, but in reviewing these particular images of long ago, even the most jaded critic is forced to admit that it all works in a way that is rarely dupli-cated today. As the expression goes, these gardens "sing."

Imagine, then, the veritable opera we heard when we first walked into the Point Ellice House garden. That roundabout tale of discovery is told in the preface. Outside the fence, you experience all the bustle and hustle of modern-day Victoria, British Columbia. Once inside the white wooden gates, however, you enter a time warp. There, gravel walks curve gracefully around trees that were planted when Queen Victoria was on the throne. Long-forgotten annuals scent the borders and musky roses dangle from house and arbor. An unbelievably smooth lawn rolls gently down to the shores of the Selkirk Water. A croquet set sits ca-sually abandoned on the grass as if the last

Inset, right: Caroline's 1855 Singer Sewing Machine. Its location in the kitchen made it accessible both to Caroline's nursemaid, who would have worked on small mending projects, as well as to any of Caroline's seamstresses who came to the O'Reilly home to work on special projects. Three serving dish covers can be seen hanging on the wall behind the machine. These food covers of plated silver kept any insects or other debris from the meal until presented at dinner.

Across, clockwise from top left: Visitors to Point Ellice today enjoy the gardens much as visitors to the house did a century ago. Then as now, fragrant plants played an important part in the O'Reilly landscape. Here, a honeysuckle, seen climbing the veranda column, as well as numerous varieties of hybrid roses, still scent the early summer air.

The gracious lawn flows from the house down to the gorge waterway, flanked by roses, arbutus, and Douglas fir.

Point Ellice House seen from the south (formerly the vegetable) garden. The large tree to the left is a hawthorn, of which Caroline O'Reilly was especially fond. The sequoia planted by Peter O'Reilly rises behind the house.

A period photograph, as well references in both Peter's and Kathleen's papers, allowed the Point Ellice curatorial and gardening staff to re-create this heart-shaped rose bed planted with nineteenth-century heirloom roses.

brougham had just carried off the final dallying guests. Here at last, was a living, breathing Victorian house and garden. This was no faded image, no print that required translation or interpretation. Point Ellice House was the real McCoy. Nor was this garden a mere re-creation; while sections of the property had been restored, the majority of the landscape had, through a bizarre combination of quirky fate and deliberate human intervention, survived intact from the Victorian era—a feat almost unique in North America. Here sat a Victorian house, with its *complete* contents, on its *original* lot, with many of its original *plantings*, and a full set of historic documentation to fill in all those pieces normally missing from the Victorian garden puzzle. In short, for a lover of the era, Point Ellice House was a dream come true.

Our interest in the place, however, was not just intellectual. Entering the Point Ellice garden was like actually being able to walk into the warm embrace of one of those old engravings with all the vivid pleasures of sight, touch, and sound restored. We were fascinated by the way the garden entranced, welcomed, bid us to enter, and enjoy. When is the last time a modern landscape had the same effect on us, we wondered. Could there be lessons here we could take back to the modern world, not just for those interested in re-creating actual Victorian gardens but also for the many of us who live in modern settings and would like to apply the theories behind these period gardens to our own landscapes? The answer to these questions is the book you have in your hands.

PETER TO CAROLINE [WRITING FROM ASHCROFT]—6 MAY 1870

I was perfectly surprised to find Mr. Cornwall's garden so forward. His lilacs are beautiful—in a few days they will be a mass of flowers and his trees don't appear to have suffered by the late frost like those at Victoria and Yale…I shall be very impatient to see your face…I miss the dear chicks more than I thought I would…

From a Victorian Garden is, to use a favorite Victorian expression, a bit of a salmagundi—a melange of information designed to give you a working knowledge not only of the Point Ellice garden but also of Victorian gardens in general, offering along the way a medley of the more interesting design elements of the period to improve your own backyard. Before we begin our journey, however, you'll need to know a little more about the times, events, and people that produced the gardens of Point Ellice House.

The Setting, Cast, and Characters

The story of the garden at Point Ellice House, like many stories in the New World, begins in the Old, with the birth of the man that would become its principal creator. Peter O'Reilly was born in Ince, Lancashire, England, in 1828 to an Irish father and an English mother. Educated at Trinity College, Dublin, he became a lieutenant in the Royal Irish Constabulary.

The Ireland of Peter O'Reilly's youth was a difficult place for an ambitious young man. The potato famine of the 1840s had caused widespread impoverishment and civil unrest, and Peter's prospects for making a substantial fortune were, at best, limited. Like so many others of that place and era, Peter began to cast around for opportunities, a search that almost inevitably led westward—in this case, five thousand miles.

Peter O'Reilly in middle age.

In what would soon become Victoria, British Columbia, Canada, the Crown Colony of Vancouver Island had been established in 1850, in part to exploit the rich natural resources claimed by the Hudson Bay Company, and in part to secure British dominion over an area threatened by the rapid territorial expansion of the nascent United States. In addition to the already well-known wealth of furs, coal, and timber found thereabouts, gold was discovered in 1857 on the mainland near the North Thompson River, north of present-day Vancouver. A gold rush quickly ensued, which led over twenty thousand miners and camp followers to sail from San Francisco—the nearest possible jumping-off point—to the completely unprepared Hudson Bay post of Fort Victoria. This massive influx absolutely swamped the minuscule resources of the tiny Crown Colony, and assistance was urgently requested from London. In response, a bill was intro-

PETER TO CAROLINE—11 APRIL 1871

How does the garden look, have you had any more cabbages planted? Don't forget to have a good supply of winter vegetables put in such as Brussels sprouts.

WHY WE GARDEN

Gardening appealed to the Victorians on many levels: as aesthetic pursuit, as social entertainment, and as a practical means of producing fresh fruit, flowers, and vegetables. One of the most important considerations for families like the O'Reillys, and one often overlooked today, was the salubrious effect gardening had both on the body and the spirit. The following testimony comes from Peter Henderson's *Gardening for Pleasure*, 1875.

About twenty years ago I had the pleasure of making the acquaintance of a gentleman whose duties compelled him to be at his desk in a close office in the city of New York, from nine o'clock A.M. to four P.M. Being naturally of a weak constitution, his sedentary life soon made him the victim of dyspepsy to such a degree that he felt that he must soon resign his situation. He was then a man of forty, entirely ignorant of anything pertaining to the country life, and it was with great misgivings and reluctance that, by the advice of his physician, he changed his home from a closely built part of New York to a cottage in the-then countrylike suburb of Jersey City Heights, New Jersey.

His means enabled him to purchase a modest cottage built on a lot fifty by one hundred and fifty feet. He did not want the land, he said, but the cottage was such as he fancied, and the ground had to go with it. It was about this time that I formed his acquaintance, through some business transaction, and he asked my professional advice as to what he could do with his land, which he had already begun to consider somewhat of an encumbrance. I replied to him that, if I was not greatly mistaken, in his little plot of land lay a cure for all his bodily ills, and that, besides, it could add to the comforts, if not the luxuries, of his table if he would only work it. "*I* work it!" he exclaimed. "You don't suppose that these hands could dig or delve," holding up his thin and bloodless fingers; "and if they could, I know nothing about gardening." I told him I thought neither objection insurmountable, if he once began.

The result of our conversation was that he resolved to try, and try he did to a purpose. Our interview was in March, and before the end of April he had his lot all nicely dug over, the labor being done by his own hands during an hour and a half each morning. His custom was to get up at six o'clock, and work at his garden until half past seven. This gave him ample time to dress, get breakfast, and be at his desk in the city by nine. The labor of merely digging was (to him) heavy and rather monotonous; but he stuck to it bravely, and when he again presented himself before me for plants and seeds, and information as to what to do with them, it was with some pride that I saw my prescription had worked so well, for my friend then looked more like a farmer than a pallid clerk.

During his first season, of course, he made some blunders and some failures, but his interest in the work increased year by year. His family was supplied with an abundance of all the fresh vegetables and fruit his limited space could admit of being grown; a supply that it would have taken at least one hundred and fifty dollars to purchase at retail, and stale at that. But the benefit derived from the cultivation of this cottage garden was health—strong, rugged health—that, for the six years he was my neighbor, never once failed him.

I know this case is an extremely exceptional one, for I never knew another man who so resolutely worked himself into health. There are hundreds of business men, book-keepers, salesmen, clerks, and the like, who live in the suburbs of all great cities, many of whom can ill afford to pay for the keeping of the plots surrounding their cottages, but who think they can far less afford to do the work themselves. As a consequence, in nine cases out of ten, the rear, at least, of their suburban plots is a wilderness of weeds. But this is not the least of the evils. The owner has a certain amount of muscular force, and this, be it more or less, being unused, its possessor pays the penalty of his laziness in dyspepsy and a host of other ills. The proofs are apparent everywhere that garden operations are conducive to health and longevity. The work is not unduly laborious, and when fairly entered into has a never-failing interest. The growing and the watching of the great variety of plants give a healthy tone to the mind, while the physical labor demanded by cultivation takes care of the body.

duced in the British House of Parliament in 1858 to create the colony of British Columbia, which, in addition to the already existing colony of Vancouver Island, encompassed what today is known as British Columbia. The two separate colonies were eventually merged in 1866 with Victoria chosen as the capital in 1868.

John Douglas was appointed the first governor of British Columbia as well as that of Vancouver Island and immediately set about creating the infrastructure and means to implement the rule of the new provincial government. A call went out for trained men to help maintain law and order, and heeding that invitation was none other than the already experienced Peter O'Reilly, who left Ireland with the obligatory letters of introduction and arrived in Victoria in 1859. There he was promptly appointed by Douglas as justice of the peace and stipendiary magistrate, a type of traveling judge. The

Caroline Trutch, before she became Mrs. Peter O'Reilly, about 1860.

term *circuit court* at the time meant exactly that—most judges were itinerant, administering justice in one seat, then moving on to the next over a set course. For most of Peter's career, he was constantly on the move—an important element in our story.

For those of you who have visited charming Victoria or cosmopolitan Vancouver recently, it is hard to imagine the transformation that has occurred in less than 150 years. In 1859, neither town officially existed. British Columbia was a wild and woolly frontier, a rugged land of trappers, miners, and other newly arrived immigrants, sorely in need of firm justice. Peter O'Reilly turned out to be just the man for the job and quickly became well known for his strict but fair hand. In one famous early instance, he gave a speech at the mining community of Wild Horse Creek in the Keetenay region of British Columbia declaring, "Now boys, there must be no shooting for if there is shooting, there will surely be hanging. . . ." In addition to these judicial roles, Peter was also appointed gold commissioner for various districts around British Columbia. Although Peter's duties required almost constant travel by boat, canoe, and horseback since roads were few and far between, and rail service to Victoria was still almost thirty years away. Nonetheless, he managed to find time to think about getting married. At a dinner party given by the Honorable Joseph Trutch, the first lieutenant governor of British Columbia, Peter met Joseph's sister, Caroline.

The daughter of William and Charlotte Hannah Trutch, Caroline was born in London, England, September 16, 1831. She arrived in British Columbia by a most roundabout fashion. Unlike Peter, who had come to Canada in search of fame and fortune, Caroline had left England in search of a suitable husband. After her extensive travels through India, Malta, and France yielded no one, she decided to accept her brother's invitation to move to British Columbia along with her mother. A handsome woman who was reported to have an astounding singing voice, Caroline must have stood out prominently in the wilds of British Columbia. She quickly caught the eye of Peter O'Reilly. A two-year courtship ensued, and finally they were married on December 15, 1863, at Christ Church Cathedral. After setting up temporary households in several of Peter's posts, the couple decided to move permanently to Victoria, principally so that Caroline could be closer to her family. Their first son, Frank, was born in 1866.

It was at this point, in 1867, that Point Ellice House enters the O'Reillys' story, or perhaps it would be better to say that the O'Reillys enter the house's story, for the structure that was to become the home of the O'Reilly family for over a hundred years had already been built. Constructed about 1861 for Charles Wentworth Wallace, the house had the distinction of having been designed by a professional architect: John Wright. One of the many pattern books available at the time may also have played a part. Certainly the house's Italianate lines have much in common with popularly published templates of the 1860s. Originally, the structure was much smaller than the building we see

Top: This is the oldest known photograph of Point Ellice House, dating from about 1870. Remnants of the primeval forest onto which the English-style house and garden were overlaid are still visible in the background. To the right of Point Ellice House is the home of Trywhitt Drake, a friend often mentioned in O'Reilly correspondence

Middle: The drawing room in Point Ellice House reveals the ornate decor the O'Reillys, and the Victorians in general, favored. Many of the furnishings date from 1880 to 1885 and were acquired by the O'Reillys on trips abroad.

Bottom: The Point Ellice House drawing room. Unlike other historic sites where the interiors were reassembled from outside sources, the possessions seen here are all original to the house. Many objects, in fact, like the watercolors on the far wall (painted by Kathleen O'Reilly herself) remain just where they were first placed a century ago.

today. Almost a cottage, it consisted of a dining room, a very small kitchen and pantry, two tiny bedrooms, and a master bedroom with dressing room, box room, study, and drawing room. Subsequent additions in 1877, 1879, 1884, 1886, and 1889 added a servant's room in the attic, along with a cellar, dormers, verandas and bay windows; expanded most of the existing rooms; and substantially altered and enlarged the service wing of the house.

The house sat in a particularly favored spot—a lovely piece of land that sloped gently down to Selkirk Water, an extension of Victoria's inner harbor. Located in what would become a very fashionable district of affluent middle-class homes about a mile from the center of town, the house was far enough removed from the city center to give it a bit of a country air, yet conveniently close to stores and services. Like the house, the lot too grew over time. In 1875, Peter was able to purchase the property adjacent to the north, expanding the grounds at Point Ellice from the original 1 acre to the 2.2 acres we still see today.

Interestingly, it almost came to pass that the O'Reillys and Point Ellice House never met. Caroline and Peter's original intention had been to rent a house on their arrival in Victoria. Caroline was pregnant again, and with Peter's constant travels,

Kathleen was photographed many times at the studios of Lambert Weston & Son in Folkstone, England. In a letter to her brother Frank in May 1884, Kathleen wrote, "I am going to send out the photos that were taken down in Folkstone of me. You will think they are very flattering." Kathleen spent three years in England at finishing school, where, among other things, she studied watercolor painting. Many of Kathleen's paintings still hang in the Point Ellice Collection.

there wasn't much time for a thorough house search. But fate intervened. As Peter writes in his diary: "December 8, received a letter from Carry informing me that the house which we were to have occupied had been burnt down." While the details of these weeks are not recorded, obviously a fairly frantic search for new quarters ensued, and somewhere in the rush, Caroline and Peter decided not to rent, but to buy, and settled at Point Ellice. The price was twenty-five hundred pounds, a not insignificant sum, considering the fact that Peter's annual salary was only eight hundred pounds a year. Peter's notes in his diary on December 12th that they "drove out to their new house got two rooms ready, and took possession." And none too soon. On the 31st of December, 1867, their daughter Kathleen, nicknamed alternately Kitty or Puss, was born at Point Ellice. Two more children would soon follow: Mary Augusta (Pop) in 1869 and Arthur John in 1873.

After Peter and Caroline, it is Kathleen who features most prominently in the history of the house and the gardens during its formative years. Although all the children gardened with their mother when young (especially the eldest, young Frank), the schooling and careers of the boys soon took them away from home. Frank and John were

From left to right: The only O'Reilly child not to survive to adulthood, Mary Augusta died painfully of spinal meningitis in 1876; Kathleen, standing in the doorway at Point Ellice and sporting a stylish riding outfit. Like many Victorians, Kathleen enjoyed riding and became an accomplished horsewoman; Kathleen O'Reilly, approximately eighteen years old, with her brothers Frank and Jack, about 1885.

CAROLINE TO PETER—18 NOVEMBER 1874

My own dear husband—The gale last night was very severe and as I sat by the warm fireside, the tears would come into my eyes when I thought of the discomfort you were suffering.... I have read your letter to the little ones — they asked me to do so and they send you much love and many kisses in return for yours. They miss you all very much. They are now having a game of play in the passage with Frederike...

largely educated in England and married English wives. Their subsequent careers and family life—Frank an engineer, who worked extensively building the Argentine railway network, and John, who studied law and was active in real estate—took them away from Point Ellice. Mary Augusta, always a sickly child, never lived to do much gardening. She died at age seven in 1876.

Kathleen, however, was different. Tutored at home until the age of thirteen, she was her mother's companion and helper, and in many ways became the second "lady of the house." While she too was sent to London for finishing school, she returned to Victoria after several years, and by and large called Point Ellice her home for the rest of her long life. She died there in 1945. Kathleen was an accomplished musician, playing both piano and harp, as well as an artist. She was fond of stitching, dance, and gardening. She was also keenly athletic, something fairly unusual for a woman of her

Kathleen O'Reilly, August 1877, photographed in a Victoria photo studio.

day, perhaps the result of growing up the only girl with two competitive brothers. Kathleen played tennis, as well as a mean game of croquet. She enjoyed boating, was a talented horsewoman, and early on took up the-then novel sports of roller skating and bicycle racing. An extremely independent spirit, she could never quite decide to give up the pleasant life she led at Point Ellice and get married. She did come close once, however, in 1892. While at Point Ellice, she had a rather protracted courtship with Captain Stanhope, the future Earl of Chesterfield, whose ship was based at the time in Victoria. Despite his enthusiasm for the match, Kathleen remained unconvinced, and Captain Stanhope sailed home to England disappointed and alone.

Interestingly, the constant travel of the O'Reillys and their Victorian contemporaries is an essential element in our story, for it produced an important key to understanding the gardens at Point Ellice. To modern readers accustomed to rapid and reasonably convenient travel, it is remarkable how peripatetic these Victorians were, voyaging back and forth across continents and oceans, despite the unpleasant rigors such travels entailed. Even today, sending a child from Vancouver to London to school would be considered no small undertaking. The Victorians, however, seemed to have thought nothing of it. For instance, when Kathleen went to school in England in 1882, she was required to take a sailing packet to San Francisco, a five-day train across the wilds of the American West to New York, then wait indefinitely for passage to London. Regularized service was yet to be a standard of Atlantic Ocean travel, and passengers were often forced to wait for days while ships accumulated sufficient passengers and cargo for the voyage. Nor were crossings without incident. Ocean travel was considered quite hazardous; etiquette guides of the time cautioned against lugubrious behavior at the quay, for fear of alarming those about to embark. On this particular trip

The Tennis Court and Balls, a painting of Point Ellice House by Kathleen O'Reilly, circa 1890. Remarkably, the modern visitor will find that the scene remains almost unchanged.

dens at Point Ellice. Victorians in general, and the O'Reillys in particular, wrote to each other constantly about their day-to-day lives—sometimes several letters a day. Nor were these letters short. Most were multiple pages of very fine script, written not only from left to right, but over again on the diagonal in order to utilize every bit of space. Mail service until the late 1800s was erratic, and postage was extremely expensive—thus every inch of paper counted.

When average trips were measured in weeks, or months, not days, mail became the only method of effective communication. In Peter's case, he supervised much of the goings-on at Point Ellice from his traveler's writing desk. Constant streams of advice, instructions urging, and admonitions flowed from his pen. He was particularly concerned with the progress of the garden, which was, by and large, his personal demesne. Peter laid out and planted much of what we see today at Point Ellice House. Caroline for her part responded with reports of the progress she made—or didn't make—tending her husband's many gardening projects; her problems with the domestics; social details; lives of the children, goings-on in Victoria—the minutiae of the family's everyday life.

Kathleen too, as she got older, wrote often to her father, noting the goings-on in the garden. Her

these fears were justified. The ship Kathleen was traveling on suffered rudder problems halfway across the Atlantic and drifted for days until rescued by another vessel. Kathleen and her mother were forced to make an extremely hazardous mid-ocean transfer to board a rescue ship, without any of their luggage. Young Kathleen recalled the whole affair as a great adventure. Caroline, though, understood the danger of the situation and was extremely relieved to arrive in England, even in their severely *mal-accoutrées* state.

Extended journeys like these, however, and the almost continuous travels required in Peter's judicial work are why we know so much about the gar-

CAROLINE TO PETER—10 APRIL 1875

I have been rendered nervous by that account of an attempted robbery at Mr. Carr's—you will see it in the paper. I am unable to get over the feeling and it makes me wakeful. This great house with so many windows and only the Chinamen. I have told Charley to keep a watch and Fung also—the latter only laughs…

Left: Harry Scudamore-Stanhope, then a lieutenant commander in the Royal Navy, courted Kathleen in the summers of 1891 and 1892. Kathleen's journal is full of references to his calling, stopping for tea, and sending bouquets. In August 1892, he finally proposed to her. Unfortunately for Scudamore-Stanhope, Kathleen declined. The two remained close friends, though, till his death many years later. Kathleen never did marry, preferring not to leave her beloved Point Ellice. *(To learn something of the language of flowers, see page 121 in the appendix.) Middle:* Mrs. Peter O'Reilly about the time she first arrived at Point Ellice. *Right:* The Honorable Peter O'Reilly, about 1903, enjoying the lawns and gardens of Point Ellice.

ever-growing artistic sensibilities, as well as her love of outdoor games, led her to take a keen interest in the flowers and grounds. It was ultimately she who took over the gardens on the death of her father in 1904. Remarkably, the O'Reillys saved almost every scrap of their correspondence—thousands and thousands of pages detailing all aspects of their lives, including a treasure trove of information about the Point Ellice House landscape. It is this correspondence, along with the family's personal diaries, and the thousands of domestic records such as gardening orders and expenses that have allowed the accu-

rate preservation, and re-creation, of today's house and gardens.

So here then begins our story. The year is 1870. The setting: a young house in the brand new capital of Victoria, British Columbia, sitting on an empty lot only recently carved out of the wilderness. The cast: Peter, up-and-coming provincial official; his wife Caroline, loyal spouse, caretaker of hearth, home, and garden, eager to assume her rightful place in Victoria society; Kathleen and the other children, poised for the future. How, then, did Peter and his family start transforming this barren, empty space into the lush landscape we see today?

GARDENERS NEARLY LOST AT SEA

Besides being an invaluable historical record, the O'Reilly correspondence also makes fascinating reading, as you will see from snippets of their letters throughout the book. To give you a better feel, though, here is an extended excerpt from one of Caroline's letters about her harrowing misadventures on the Atlantic. Needless to say, had events turned out differently, there might have been no gardens at Point Ellice to welcome us today.

Lambert Weston & Son   FOLKESTONE

Liverpool
15 May 1882

My own beloved husband,
No words can tell our thankfulness for our deliverance from the danger we were in! . . . We had had fine weather and the *Catalonia* made good progress from New York until Sunday the seventh, when suddenly about 4 P.M. the shaft broke—there was a fearful noise and the ship trembled so it seemed as if she was being torn to pieces. The steam was turned off and then it seemed as if the boiler would burst! All was horror! At first the officers said there was not much damage, but finally the Captain sent word to the passengers that the shaft was broken, that nothing could be done and that we must proceed under sail! The weather, as I stated before, was very fine so there was no immediate danger (provided the ship had not been injured when the accident occurred and this they assured us was the case!) But what a prospect: Nineteen hundred miles from Liverpool and contrary winds against us should we attempt to return to New York! . . .

Sunday evening passed and the whole of Monday and the ship made no progress. It became apparent that she had little or no sailing capacity!! Monday night I felt very

anxious. . . . On Tuesday Morning the 9th we were roused by hearing the glad tidings that a steamer lay along side and that she would receive the passengers and take them on to Liverpool. It was 4 A.M., but we got up at once, packed up with haste and went on deck. The steamer proved to be the *Sarmatiau* of the Allan Line. She had over 70 passengers but was able to accommodate 150: we, however, were 90, besides steerage! She took us all, however, and brought us safely to Liverpool.

The morning we were transferred was wonderfully calm for the Atlantic, but still it was a trial of courage to go in an open boat (small) with 4 oars (and crowded with passengers) from one ship to the other. We had to go down the ship's side with a rope ladder, and the *Catalonia* is 5000 tons burden so you may think how high she is out of the water! It was easier to get on board the *Sarmatiau*—she is 3000 tons and has a stairway that is let down. After we were on board there was great difficulty in finding accommodation but of this I must tell you later—The *Sarmatiau* took the disabled ship in tow and proceeded bravely on her way—towed her 240 miles out of danger of the icebergs, for we then learned that we had become disabled just in their track!! You can realise now the danger we were in! . . .

CHAPTER I
DESIGNING A VICTORIAN GARDEN

The Victorian Garden Defined • Tabula Rasa • Essential Elements of a Victorian Garden • Rooms with a View

The Importance of Taking Stock • Fences and Hedges • PLANTS WITH A PAST: Holly

The Victorian Garden Defined

So what makes a garden Victorian? Perhaps the most distinguishing element of the gardens of this period, especially when compared to landscapes today, is the quality of their design—the way in which the house and the garden act as a single unit. When you arrive at a house like Point Ellice, you immediately sense that the landscape embraces the architecture, linking it to the land, like a rose gently twining up a delicate arbor. In fact, the Victorian preference for the term *home grounds*, when describing house and garden, underscores the association between architecture and nature. This stands in great contrast to modern landscapes, which, even when well designed in and of themselves, often appear divorced from the buildings that stand in their midst. This dichotomy is even more evident when the landscape has been put together piecemeal over a large number of years in response to changing whims of different owners. The result is often a hodgepodge of unrelated elements that entirely ignore one another and the house. Nothing could have been further from the Victorian ideal.

Victorian landscapes were also preeminently social. In many ways, they were like stage sets for lucky homeowners and their privileged guests to act out an endless series of entertainments—luncheons and teas, lawn games, fetes, elaborate outdoor dinners, or merely intimate strolls. In this modern age of air-conditioned quarters, when many people's only contact with the outdoors in the summer is commuting to and from work, it's hard for us to remember that for a large portion of the year, the garden was the *only* cool place around. People lived in their gardens during the warm summer months. Victorian gardens were used daily, intensively, and their design reflected that use. Gardens were laid out to hold something in reserve, to encourage a sense of exploration and mystery. Views were framed and expanded, paths deliberately curved to hide their ends, beds of scented flowers located at unexpected turns, all to delight and distract the visitor. In the same way we might value our TV or stereo, gardens were a source of relaxation and entertainment in a much quieter age.

Perhaps most important, Victorian gardens were expected to be productive as well as aesthetically pleasing. With their love of newly discovered annuals and unusual shrubs and trees from exotic lands, Victorians invented the modern ornamental landscape, and would be appalled to the extent that modern gardens have abandoned any semblance of productivity. During the Victorian era, most families depended on their lots to produce a large portion of the fruit and vegetables they consumed over the course of the year, especially in winter. Even near large urban centers, where food concerns were less pressing, no self-respecting homeowner would consider even a largely ornamental landscape to be complete without at least a

The Victorian ideal of the garden: nature tamed for the benefit, and edification, of man.

For the Victorians, the landscape was simply an extension of the indoors outside: the garden as a summer parlor of sorts, designed to entertain and amuse.

few grape vines, an apple tree, or a plot of spring greens.

So these were the goals of the O'Reillys: to create unified home grounds where house, garden, and nature all worked together as one; to furnish a beautiful setting for relaxation and social entertainment; and to provide a productive yet aesthetically pleasing source of fresh fruit and vegetables for the home. Yet where to begin?

Tabula Rasa

As the chief architect of the gardens at Point Ellice House, Peter O'Reilly faced a situation in the spring of 1870 that is familiar to many modern homeowners: a newly constructed house sitting on a barren lot, completely exposed to the road and the neighbors with few, if any, trees, no flowers, fruit trees, or lawn. In short, he had a blank slate, a tabula rasa, which was in desperate need of some landscaping. Given the number of gardening books and periodicals still found in the Point Ellice House collection, Peter most likely began by doing what many do today, educating himself with a good book. By the 1860s, home gardening guides were becoming common: Shirley Hibberd, Joseph Breck, and Jane Webb Loudon had produced works on both sides of the Atlantic aimed at the newly emerging middle-class "villa gardener." One of the most influential of these books, both with homeowners and with other garden authors of the time, was Edward Kemp's *How to Lay Out a Small Garden*, first published in 1850 and reprinted again and again for almost sixty years. Whether Peter O'Reilly had access to this particular work, or whether he merely absorbed the information from other tastemakers of the period is not known, but it is pretty clear that Peter O'Reilly was following the most current and fashionable advice offered by books like Kemp's when he laid out the grounds at Point Ellice.

Top: A view of Peter's desk, with Henderson's best-selling *Gardening for Profit*, one of the many period horticultural books still found at the house. It was guides like this one that helped Peter O'Reilly shape the gardens at Point Ellice.

Bottom: The O'Reilly book collection includes many garden and flower guides as well as the personal selections of each family member. Here Kathleen's books remain on her bedroom shelf, as if she had just left the room.

Essential Elements of a Victorian Garden

The first thing Peter had to do was decide which elements he wanted to include in his new garden. Certain ones of course were mandatory, just as they would be today. Every house needed a service area; for example, an access drive to the carriage house or barn, housing for the horse and carriage, a place for the cow, room for some chickens, and storage for tools. These were generally located near the more utilitarian section of the house, and away from the social areas. Thus it's no surprise that Peter assigned the barnyard and working area to the north side of the lot—the side nearest the kitchen and the least productive horticulturally.

Equally important to a Victorian family would be a kitchen garden. Year-round access to store-bought fruit and vegetables was many years in the future, and many Victorian families, especially those outside of urban areas, relied on what they could grow themselves. To be successful, however, kitchen gardens required good light and soil, and at Point Ellice, the southern boundary of the lot, although rather distant from the kitchen, offered by far the best location for growing. This left the east (front) and west (rear of the house) for ornamental and recreational uses. To the socially conscious Victorians, these were perhaps the most important areas of all.

Rooms with a View

Maintaining proper appearances was of paramount importance to advancing one's career in Victorian society, and ambitious men like Peter O'Reilly knew it. But he was in somewhat of a quandary, for while his salary was certainly comfortable, his income was insufficient to make the major additions to the Point Ellice living quarters that his growing social status would have otherwise called for. However, Peter understood a design concept that is often overlooked today. If thoughtfully done, you can make a property seem much more spacious than it is by designing gracious outdoor living areas that complement and expand the house's indoor functions. In designing these areas, however, a restrained hand was often called for. It was very easy to overdo.

Possibly the greatest and most prevalent mistake of those who layout a garden for themselves is attempting too much. One thing after another is at different times observed and liked, in some place visited, and each is successively wished to be transferred to the observer's own garden, without regard to what has been previously done. The practice of cutting up a garden into mere fragments, which is

The sun was very hot and I could not put out the plants I brought down until the evening. I had also to put out those sent down by Mrs. Dewdney which I found need not been undone, only standing in a bucket of water. Amongst them was an acacia (small) but with a beautiful root. I have put it in the vegetable garden under the hedge and also the root cuttings Mrs. D. sent as I thought they would stand a better chance there. She also sent 4 gladiolus roots—I assure you I could not have finished…if Rose's husband had not helped me.…I am so glad the wisteria is actually growing. I was very tired but I persevered till all were planted and you can think how much I missed you, dear one, and how lonely I felt tho the little man [son Frank] is a great talker and worker…

unhappily of too frequent occurrence, is the natural result of such a state of things.

—EDWARD KEMP,
How to Lay Out a Small Garden

Heeding this advice, Peter limited his choices. The front yard was to be transformed into a gracious and stately approach to the house. With a curved gravel drive and ornamental shrubbery beds, it would become a de facto extension of the front hall and dining room. In the rear he opted to create a large, sweeping games lawn bordered by flowers and looking out over the water. Not only would the area be perfect for the-then wildly popular sports of lawn tennis and croquet, but the social opportunities such games afforded could not but increase his family's social connections and standing.

Having blocked out these areas in his mind's eye, Peter then needed to figure out how to define these spaces. Then, as now, every distinct area of the garden required some sort of boundary to make it effective, in the same way that a room needs walls to define its size and limits, or a picture needs a frame to define its borders. Before the Victorian era, hedges and fences had been extensively used to delineate areas of the garden and were still fairly common sights in the home landscape. Walls, such as stone or brick, were another common means of defining space; but they weren't used at Point Ellice. By the 1830s, however, there had been some new thinking on the subject, and substantial changes were afoot.

THE IMPORTANCE OF TAKING STOCK

Before even a single shovel of dirt has been moved or a single branch cut down, it is imperative to take *very* careful stock of what you already have. Before you can see the true result of any future landscape renovations, you need to understand completely what currently works and what doesn't; what is growing well and what isn't; what's present, or what may be, and what is not. This is especially true in old gardens, where many a garden ghost may be lurking about. This is exactly what occurred at Point Ellice House during the 1980s. When the house was first turned over to the province of British Columbia, the site was carefully surveyed and mapped out by a dedicated group of architects, archaeologists, and historians who charted the current state of the existing landscape down to the last tree, bush, and flower. What they found surprised them greatly. Not only were a large number of specimen plants still thriving from the time of the O'Reillys but many other previously unknown plants were still hanging on to life buried under mounds of scrub and ivy. Fragments of iron fencing were found buried in limbs, which allowed for the restoration of an entire fence line; bits of trellis revealed long-forgotten arbors; pathways emerged from under 1960s sod. If a wholesale restoration had taken place before this careful investigation had been completed, many wonderful elements of the garden we see today might have been lost.

Of course, in a house-museum setting with a trained professional staff, this is relatively easy to do. The average homeowner however, faces a much more daunting task. If your current landscape is generally simple and straightforward, often a pencil, some graph paper, a good identification guide (or the computerized version thereof), plus a good nose for detail are all that is needed to produce a decent overall chart of what exists there. If your grounds are extensive, or contain a large number of puzzling specimens, professional design help may be required. Hiring a professional is a particularly good idea if you are uncertain about important design details, or are unsure about the condition of major horticultural specimens. There is, for instance, no use planning a terrace around an ancient oak with a hollow, decayed center. When in doubt, ask for help; any amount spent now will be more than recompensed down the line. *For advice on laying out your yard, see page 106 in the appendix.*

Fences and Hedges

The Victorians knew, like their gardening predecessors, that the design of the fence can make or break a garden. As an extension of the architecture of the house into the landscape, it was crucial that a fence match the style and feel of the house. As the century wore on, however, additional concerns presented themselves. As Frank Scott notes in *Suburban Home Grounds:*

> For large suburban grounds, it is safe to say that except where hedges are maintained, the kind of fence is best which is least seen, and best seen through. But in town, our fences must harmonize with the architecture and more elegant finish of the street, and therefore be sufficiently well-designed and constructed to be in themselves pleasing objects to the passerby. The great desideratum is to answer this requirement, and at the same time adopt some design that will least conceal the lawn and other beauties beyond or behind it. Our fences, should be so to speak, transparent.

It's not surprising then that when Peter constructed the fence along Pleasant Street, he followed this formula almost exactly. The intricate, white wooden structure, borrowing design details from the house, had a sufficiently grand weight and feel to give a distinguished air to the place, yet was welcoming enough in scale and style not to overwhelm the single-story house or intimidate a guest. The ample pickets, set widely apart, clearly defined the limits of the garden, while still allow-

Kathleen and her horse Blackie at the front gate.

ing the passerby a view of the lovely house and garden beyond.

The Victorians also had some very specific ideas on that other means of dividing space—hedges. Unlike fences, which can be made more or less transparent, hedges generally tend toward dense growth. While this was considered a valuable asset for working areas of the landscape such as the kitchen garden, or for areas around "necessaries" or outbuildings that were generally removed from public view, ornamental areas were a different story altogether. Hedges, especially ones with any height, were to be thoroughly banished. Take Mr. Scott in *Suburban Home Grounds:*

> The practice of hedging one's ground so that the passerby cannot enjoy its beauty, is one of the barbarisms of old gardening, as absurd and unchristian in our day as the walled courts and barred windows of a Spanish cloister, and as

needlessly aggravating as the closed veil of Egyptian women.

Or Mr. Kemp in *How to Lay Out a Small Garden:*

> [Hedges] serve in fact completely to shut the garden in by a kind of green wall, which effectually excludes a great deal of sunlight and air and all appearance of distance. They make the garden a sort of prison which cannot be seen into by others and from which not a glimpse can be obtained of what is passing without. Privacy no doubt they may secure, but it is the privacy of the cell or the cloister—a sort of monastic seclusion which would better fit the tenant of a hermitage.

A glimpse of the gardens from the front gate.

Strong words indeed, and woe be the poor gardener who failed to heed this advice. Perhaps as a direct consequence of such counsel, at Point Ellice, hedges are used in a limited fashion. A laurel hedge separates the working kitchen garden from the rest of the landscape, and a hedge of low-clipped holly provides a backing for the planting in the center of the carriage drive.

Given the force of these admonitions, a word or two should probably be added for the modern gardener who may note that he or she faces a very different situation from the Victorians. While the average house 120 years ago generally fronted onto what to today's eyes seem fairly bucolic lanes subject only to the passing of the occasional horse, the twenty-first-century homeowner more often than not faces a busy road choked with automobile traffic or is party to some view that is better left unseen. The Victorians acknowledged that special situations could occur to necessitate the need for a thick barrier. In such cases, however, it was important not to plant a uniform line of single species, at least in ornamental areas of the garden.

> There are extremely few places so thoroughly surrounded by bad objects as to allow of no breaks in the boundary and no peeps into the country beyond. And even where such is the case considerable diversity and interest may be created by the use of plants of different heights and habits to act as the screen. Indeed a boundary that must necessarily be a barrier to all further view into the outlying country may be so contrived and treated as scarcely to appear like a boundary at all.

—EDWARD KEMP,
How to Lay Out a Small Garden

For tips on hedges and border screens and a list of period shrubs for hedging, see pages 108–9 in the appendix. For information on how to espalier trees to use as a possible "fence," see page 126 in the appendix.

Perhaps the most prominent plants in the front yard of Point Ellice House are the massive English hollies that grace the carriage drive. The O'Reillys probably planted them shortly after their arrival. One can imagine that the sight of their dark, evergreen leaves provided a comfortably nostalgic link to the gardens they remembered in Britain. Interestingly, their inclusion also connected the Point Ellice garden with ancient traditions dating back thousands of years.

Holly has been important in Western gardens almost since the dawn of recorded history. The Druids, the ancient sect that built such monuments as Stonehenge, believed that the sun never abandoned the holly bush, and revered it as a symbol of the eternal turn and return of the seasons. The Romans held that the plant was sacred to the god Saturn, whose festival, Saturnalia, fell in late December and was eventually subsumed into the Christian celebration of Christmas. During the feast, Romans sent boughs and wreaths of holly to friends as a token of goodwill. They considered the plant a powerful counter charm, as did many Native American tribes, and branches of holly were commonly hung about the house and stables to protect the occupants from evil spirits around the time of the solstice. This was the birth of our holiday holly customs.

The Roman naturalist Pliny the Elder also noted that holly planted beside one's home was equally potent to ward off malicious enchantments, as well as stray bolts of lightning. Was Peter O'Reilly aware of this when he placed his bushes so prominently near the front entrance? Holly also featured prominently in the divination lore of many cultures. In medieval England, for example,

HOLLY

holly was the center of various spells used by maidens to predict what their future husband would be like. Walking sticks carved of holly were, until the end of the Victorian era, quite in demand. Not only was the wood fine and strong but holly was also thought to give protection against wild beasts and mad dogs, a belief dating back to at least the sixth century B.C., when Pythagoras recorded it.

While holly walking sticks may no longer be *le dernier cri*, planting holly still is, and no good garden should be without some member of the holly clan. The holly family (the genus *Ilex*) is huge, with species native to every continent except Antarctica, offering literally thousands of varieties to choose from. One of the largest groups, and perhaps the most famous, are the English hollies, *Ilex aquifolium*, like those at Point Ellice. The name literally means "spiky-leaved hollies" and is quite apt. The armed, curly foliage is noteworthy for its extremely glossy, dark green leaves. Many different variegated patterns, both silver and gold, have also been bred, and have been popular since the Victorian era. The large berries, which turn color in the late fall, can be either red or yellow.

Native to southern and western Europe, *Ilex aquifolium* will eventually form a pyramidal-shaped small tree, some varieties reaching as high as seventy-five feet at maturity. The specimens at Point Ellice have been carefully pruned and rejuvenated to return them to a more historically accurate scale. English holly's main drawback is its limited range—Zones 6B to 8A. Kept too cold, the plant winter kills. If it's too warm, it rots. But where it thrives, English holly is spectacular. Other varieties, such as the Merserve hollies (*Ilex meserveae*) are quite similar and more cold hardy. Used singly, English hollies make excellent specimens in the landscape and can also be espaliered or topiaried. Massed, they create an almost impenetrable screen or hedge.

CHAPTER II

MAKING IT ALL WORK TOGETHER

Buried Bones

When asked to name the most important element of a successful garden, most people would answer the plants. But this is not the case. Mere plants don't a garden make. In fact, plants can be compared to the icing on a cake. The last element to be installed when a garden is built, plants are really the *decorations*, not the substance, of the garden. Victorians like the O'Reillys knew that the most important part of any particular landscape is what's referred to as the *bones* of the garden, the nonliving portion of the grounds—the bricks, mortar, gravel, wood, and other hardscape features that make up the permanent part of the landscape. Like bones, these serve to link and support the structure as a whole. If you think about it for a moment, you can see why this would be the case. Even in a fairly mild climate like the Zone 8 garden at Point Ellice, there is a portion of the year when the plants aren't in bloom, or for some, even in leaf. During these times, when the flesh is stripped away, visual interest in the landscape is maintained by the bones. It is the hardscaping that furnishes visual logic to the overall landscape by providing reference points and access routes that link the various portions together. This is particularly true of the most prominent and ubiquitous aspect of the hardscape—paving.

> Taste demands that there should be a perfect harmony between the various portions of a garden both with respect to each other and to its buildings. . . . The transitions in it should all be easy and flowing, the lines all graceful, the decorations elegant. Its forms and figures ought all to be gently rounded off, and unite softly with each other. Lawn and gravel, shrub tree and flower, with all the less common and more costly appendages, must appear to belong to one another, and to fit into the place in which they occur.
>
> —EDWARD KEMP,
> *How to Lay Out a Small Garden*

Winding Ways to Success

When well located, walks and drives convey the idea of habitableness, imparting an air of welcome and freedom to a home and grounds, and in no slight degree seem to promote the beauty of the place. The most important walks and drives are those at the entrance . . . Architects ask that a house be thus seen to show it at its best. We should aim to make the first view of a residence and grounds as favorable as possible.

—ELIAS A. LONG,
Ornamental Gardening for Americans

The Victorians lavished tremendous attention on their walks and drives, and at Point Ellice the wonderful gravel paths and drives that meander through the grounds are striking. By and large, these paths, which date from the time of the O'Reillys, have been meticulously restored by the curatorial staff using period construction methods to serve two functions—as all well-designed paths and drives do. They are both a practical means of entrance and egress, as well as an aesthetic link between the various areas of the gardens. While the practical value of paths and drives remains important to today's gardener, the aesthetics are another matter entirely. Often nowadays, walks and drives are laid down without much thought about how the paving moves through the landscape, or what impact they will have on the look of the garden as a whole. As a result a side or front yard begins to resemble a suburban-mall parking lot. Obviously, this should not be the goal. In the same way that it is important that fences match the design and feel of the house, it's critical that sufficient time, energy, and effort be invested in garden paths and drives to be sure that they match the overall style of the garden as a whole.

Victorian gardening manuals abound with extensive advice on making paths and drives. Like those at Point Ellice House, most paths and drives consisted of crushed stone and gravel, which was the staple of Victorian landscapes. Solid surfacing such as brick and stone was actually quite rare outside of major urban areas, due to the high cost of transport. Concrete and asphalt, never particularly appropriate to the garden setting, didn't become common until well after the turn of the century. Unlike today's gravel paths, however, Victorian paths were quite elaborately constructed, using multiple layers of crushed stone and gravel, with the coarsest material on the bottom, rising

Clematis and jasmine welcome visitors to the front doorway of Point Ellice House in this view circa 1900. Immediately to the left of the door is the famous Fremontia, growing between Peter and Caroline's bedroom window and the front porch. Peruvian lilies as well as other annuals and potted geraniums provided a dash of color during the summer months.

through more finely grained material at the top. This layering technique produced an extremely hard, durable surface that drained quickly even in the wettest weather, an important consideration in a rainy climate like that of Victoria.

A visitor to Point Ellice House would have noticed another characteristic uncommon to today's garden path. The gravel was unusually flat and smooth because the O'Reilly paths were frequently rolled. Rollers, like Peter's large cast-iron example, which still exists at Point Ellice, were a common feature in period landscapes. The Victorians liked things flat and that included both lawns and pathways, which were commonly rolled after heavy rains. At Point Ellice House, archival evidence exists to show that the gardeners frequently weeded, raked, and rolled the gravel paths to maintain their fresh appearance.

Revealing the merest glimpse of the croquet lawn in the background, the gravel walk in the south garden hints of pleasures to come.

Not only do the walks and drives of Point Ellice House blend into the landscape, but they also provide an easy access to pass from one area of the garden to another. To a large degree, this has to do with the ample way that Peter O'Reilly chose to lay out his paths and drives. Take the main carriage drive for instance. The semicircular loop, neatly edged with rounded river stones (locally called cobbles but not to be confused with the squarish blocks we commonly see today) is the main feature of the front landscape. Its sinuous curves, twelve feet wide, generously invite visitors to the prominent front entrance and bid them a gracious adieu when they leave. This is a very different story from most modern driveways, which as a general rule are purely practical creations, with as much aesthetic charm as a downtown expressway. The Victorians firmly believed in combining grace with utility, and one of the ways they achieved this was by paying close attention to how the line of walks and drives moved through the landscape.

Straight lines were not unheard of, especially in small urban gardens where space was restricted, or in purely practical areas like the kitchen gardens at Point Ellice, but at larger sites, Victorian walks and drives were generally governed by the eye.

CAROLINE TO PETER—25 APRIL 1875

The garden looks very nice, the flowers are still in beautiful bloom. The sweet peas are showing in several places and I fancy one of the May trees near the well is covered with coming blossoms — it is the one with two stems — I will not fail to keep and send you some of the blossoms …

Top, left: Seen from the carriage house, the wide, welcoming drive offers a view of the front lawn.

Top, right: Honeysuckle and climbing roses frame the path that leads from the house to the croquet lawn.

Left: Kathleen, standing on the gracefully curved walkway bordering the house and croquet lawn. One of the most fascinating aspects of the Point Ellice gardens is the number of plant survivors from the time of the O'Reillys. For instance, around the corner from where Kathleen is standing in this turn-of-the-last-century photo, a jasmine reaches to just below roofline, and still grows there today. To Kathleen's right is another survivor—one of the original lilac bushes rejuvenated by the curators in the 1980s.

Laid out in pleasant bends and curves, they always made sure, however, that there was some apparent reason for the deviation, even if one had to be created through artificial props like evergreen plantings. So fond, in fact, were the Victorians of these curves that as the century wore on, tastemakers of the day were forced to speak out against the practice of making too many unnecessary deviations. Fortunately, at Point Ellice House, Peter O'Reilly didn't succumb to overly sinuous temptations, and all his paths flow in easy curves that take the visitor comfortably and conveniently from one location to another in the garden. This should be the goal in your garden as well.

Paving Possibilities

The first step to achieving aesthetically pleasing walks and drives is to stop thinking of them as solely practical elements of the landscape, ugly but necessary, when in fact they should be valuable additions to the overall appearance of your yard. Your choice of surfacing is important. It is crucial to select a surface that won't fight with the rest of your landscape. At Point Ellice, gravel was the obvious choice. It was relatively inexpensive, readily available, and went well with the fairly naturalistic style of the garden as a whole. While gravel is often the most appropriate material for many historic homes, it does require maintenance and upkeep. Often other materials will work just as well if not better, depending on what other materials are common in your area. If your house is made of brick, by all means experiment with using brick. If your landscape is rocky, stone may be a good choice. For an area near the shore, crushed oyster shells or sea stones set in mortar would work well.

The important idea is to make sure that the paving surfaces contribute to the year-round interest of the property. By all means, avoid using deadly black asphalt or ugly unadorned concrete; however, even these unimaginative surfaces can be made more interesting by adding aggregates to the mix to produce a mottled, stony surface. Asphalt, in fact, can be overlaid with tar and gravel to create a surface that very much resembles gravel. Whichever you choose, don't forget to edge the borders. Paths and borders with clearly defined edges will add a clean and tidy look to the landscape throughout the entire year.

Lawn, Shrubs, and Trees

If you accept the Victorian metaphor of the landscape as a series of distinct outdoor rooms with the hardscaping forming the walls, floors, and doorways, then it's easy to visualize the next step

CAROLINE TO PETER—17 MAY 1871

The lawn and the garden are looking very pretty. The stock and the wallflowers in full bloom perfume the air and I have been very busy putting out the geraniums, sowing seeds and weeding.

in the building process of ornamenting the room with furniture of trees and shrubs and carpets of lawns. Before you begin this last part, however, you need to understand the Victorian concept of the lawn, which is very different from our own.

We live in a day and age where the lawn has emerged as the premier feature of many gardens. In many places, in fact, the lawn has *become* the garden. In the United States, we spend more on lawns and lawn care than any other aspect of our landscape. Although the Victorians were equally concerned about the appearance of their lawns, their efforts in creating them were directed to an entirely different end. A good lawn was required not as an ornament in itself, but to provide a verdant canvas upon which to show off the principal decorations of the garden—the trees, shrubs, and flowers, which were the true heart of the garden. The fact that it also made a perfect surface for entertainment was a happy bonus.

Trees, shrubs, lawn, and drive all combine here to form one of the front garden "rooms" at Point Ellice.

Placement of the lawn was a fairly easy proposition. Like a fine rug, it was simply laid down to adorn the empty spaces between major structural elements of the landscape. At Point Ellice, the lawn areas occur chiefly in the front circle along the carriage drive, which complements the house and streetside planting. In the back the lawns provide an open place from which to appreciate the gardens and the views beyond. Placement of the "furniture," the trees, shrubs, and flowers on this living "rug," however, was a much more complicated proposition, and Victorian gardening books go to great lengths to describe the proper ways to ornament the lawn.

To understand how the Victorians placed plants in their gardens, it's important to realize that once again there has been a sea change in how we view our landscapes. These days, more often than not we choose plants for exceedingly utilitarian purposes. A large conifer may block an unpleasant view, shrubs may hide an ugly foundation, or a large tree might shade a hot terrace. Utilitarianism above all. Even purely ornamental portions of the landscape, like perennial borders, often function as a means to an end. While Victorian gardeners were certainly concerned with practicalities too, by and large Victorian gardens were much more decorative than we are accustomed to today. Part of the reason was because trees, shrubs, and flowers were chosen not only for

PETER TO CAROLINE—11 AUGUST 1874

The mower should be oiled and run over the croquet lawn at once, and at least once a week. And don't forget to have the trees and shrubs well watered.

ANIMALS AT POINT ELLICE

CAROLINE TO PETER—14 MAY 1871

The hens do not lay so many eggs now but we still get about 4 a day and that is sufficient for the three children and Mama to have a fresh one every day. We have three hens sitting on 13 eggs each and after that we shall not let any more sit. There are only twelve chicks left out of the first setting but things are doing well and all go into the Fowl house every night to sleep which is being brought up in the right way. . . . Tom [one of the Chinese servants] takes great care of the horse and as to the cow he is miserable because I won't let him cut the grass in the field for her. I tell him that she can get plenty of feed outside now and the bye and bye when the feed is scarce she can be put in the field. He (Tom) makes delicious butter and is quite put out if we ask for any cream! We had so much butter we could not want it all so the baker has had 11 pounds at 30 cents a pound and that will nearly pay his month's bill, but of course, that won't last long.

CAROLINE TO PETER—4 NOVEMBER 1872

Friday night I had little rest . . . your black friend "Tom" and another cat made the most fearful howling I ever heard. I had to get up and drive them out of the porch where they had established themselves. . . .

KATHLEEN TO PAPA—8 JULY 1878

The day before yesterday another brood of chickens came out; the hen had her nest somewhere and they are running about the yard.

KATHLEEN'S DIARY—12 MARCH 1887

Alice Ward and I had to chase cows off the tennis court. . . . I found Father and Mother in the garden . . .

Although not considered part of the garden today, animals were an essential element of the Victorian landscape. Besides supplying food for the family and manure for the garden, animals and all the paraphernalia needed to raise and maintain them often determined the layout of the grounds. Even relatively urban landscapes like the 2½ acre lot of the O'Reillys would have contained a wide assortment of furry and feathered friends. In addition to the dogs and cats that lived in the house along with Kathleen's pet canary, the O'Reillys kept chickens for meat; hens for eggs; an old pet gobbler; cows, (usually 1 or 2 at a time to provide milk and butter); and of course at least 2 horses either to ride or to pull the carriage. The larger farm-type animals lived in the large barn on the property and used the field across the street for forage. The rest were accommodated in the assortment of other smaller buildings like the carriage shed and henhouse that were scattered along the north side of the property. On many days, such a menagerie must have made for a rather riotous and amusing garden scene!

The first barn built on the property had fallen into disrepair by the late 1870s, and Peter decided to have a new one built. In his diary Peter notes on February 19, 1879 that he had decided to give "Franklin The Contract to build The Stable for $510.00 to be finished in 21 days." It was on March 31, 1879 that Peter wrote again in his diary . . . "Jack led the first horse, Joe, into the new stable." The 1879 structure is shown here before its reconstruction in the 1990s to be used as a curatorial office and visitor reception center/gift shop.

Left: Peonies, English bluebells, and tulips form delicate patches of color in the springtime flower beds.

Right: Notice how the laurel and lilac shown have been carefully pruned to prevent them from overwhelming the house behind. The Victorian considered shrubs like these located near the foundation to be ornaments, not detriments, to the architecture.

their function, but also as objects of art. The idea of plants as specimens to be noticed and admired was very much the mind-set of the times. Interesting foliage color or leaf shape, unusual habit, or pure novelty were all considered ample justifications for inclusion in the landscape.

Remember that the nineteenth century was a time of tremendous change in the garden. Beginning in the 1840s, huge advances in hybridization, combined with numerous collecting expeditions to all corners of the globe, resulted in an incredible influx of new plants into the Victorian garden. Even the more modest landscape gardens soon began to bulge with exotic introductions, and the

O'Reillys were hardly immune. The giant sequoia in the woodland garden, the Fremontia on the front wall of the house, the latest and newest in roses and annuals in the borders all attest to the collecting interest of the O'Reillys. The zest for novelty, however, had a distinct downside. Many gardeners succumbed to the tendency to try to cram their gardens with as many specimens as possible, and shortly after the Civil War, warnings against such excess became common in Victorian gardening guides. Trees, shrubs, and flower beds should not simply be randomly placed in the lawn, they warned. Artful composition was required, and fortunately the O'Reillys followed such good advice, like these three tips from Long in *Ornamental Gardening for Americans:*

Ornamenting the Lawn

1. *Let it be noted at the outset, that the partly open feature of a landscape is most essential, if we would have beautiful gardens. The open area affords a field for viewing the garden-beauty, a space for admitting cool breezes and sunshine; a play ground for shadow, and then, most important of all, that degree of general repose and breath, without which no garden can be satisfactory.*

The open lawn spaces, these "play grounds for shadow" are one of the most distinctive features of the Point Ellice landscape. Unencumbered by plantings, they were clearly designed to enhance the experience of the garden with views across the property to the vistas beyond.

Holly, lilac, laurel, and lavender (from left to right, seen here off the front carriage drive) illustrate the Victorian's love of combining interesting texture and color into their shrubbery groupings.

2. *In employing trees and shrubs for ornament, such a selection should be aimed at ensuring the greatest possible degree of beauty and interest attainable. The right idea in the garden is to bring together such kinds of trees and shrubs as possess contrasting qualities. Beautiful effects spring from combining differently tinted species and varieties of the same genus: for instance: the light and dark spruces, pines, and others, may be contrasted with one another, and so on with different kinds indefinitely.*

In general, these groupings were designed with the largest or most visually massive material toward the center, with lighter and lower material toward the edges. The chief idea was to pair and contrast plants effectively with complementary colors, textures, and shapes. The groupings, incidentally, were the answer to the objections commonly raised against hedging. Need to screen an unpleasant view in an ornamental area of the garden? Rather than a straight line of a single species, natural looking plantings of mixed shrubs were the preferred method for creating boundaries in the ornamental areas of the garden.

3. *In the matter of general style and location of groups, it is obvious, as we consider the importance of retaining certain open stretches of lawn, that as a rule the masses must, in all small spaces, be set along the margins of the grass plat, keeping the center open. In all fair sized places, the boundary masses may jut inwards to a considerable distance here and there, and some isolated clumps*

ON GARDEN ORNAMENT

One of the most interesting features of the Point Ellice garden is its almost total lack of garden adornments. Several simple wooden benches, a number of iron rose arbors, and a sundial (of dubious historical authenticity) are all that constitute the garden's decorations. Perhaps Peter O'Reilly had this advice in mind when undertaking such a spartan approach:

Kathleen O'Reilly relaxing in a corner of the croquet lawn with a book and a dog. In keeping with the easygoing, natural style of the gardens, ornamentation was kept to a minimum at Point Ellice, and garden seating consisted of portable wicker or wooden chairs and benches.

A garden may also be overloaded with a variety of things which, though ornamental in themselves, and not at all out of keeping with the house, or the principal elements of the landscape, may yet impart to it an affected or ostentatious character. An undue introduction of sculpture or other figures, vases, seats and arbors, baskets for plants, and such like objects, will come within the limits of this description. And there is nothing of which people in general are so intolerant in others, as the attempt, when glaringly and injudiciously made, to crowd within a confined space the appropriate adornments of the most ample garden. It is invariably taken as evidence of a desire to appear to be and to possess that which the reality of the case will not warrant, and is visited with the reprobation and contempt commonly awarded ill-grounded assumption. An unpresuming garden, like a modest individual, may have great defects without challenging criticism; and will even be liked and praised because of its very unobtrusiveness. But where a great deal is attempted, and there is much of pretension, whether in person or things, scrutiny seems invited, incongruities are magnified, and actual merits are passed by unnoticed, or distorted into something quite ridiculous.

—EDWARD KEMP,
How to Lay Out a Small Garden

be introduced for creating minor vistas. It is the special merit of the grouping system that it tends to give an enlarged idea of the size of the place. Grounds with the boundaries shut off by masses, and those arranged with irregular outlines, will *look larger than they would if the boundary lines were plainly in sight.*

You only need to step into the Point Ellice garden to appreciate how this last idea works. As you walk through the garden, it is hard to believe that such an entire landscape is contained within two acres. This effect was achieved by cleverly placing undulating groups of shrubs and trees to extend views where desirable and block those that were not.

Foundation Plantings, or Lack Thereof

Before we leave the subject of placing trees and shrubs, a word or two about the large heavy plantings we so often see in front of houses today. This is a design concept that would have been completely foreign to the Victorians. The first and most important tenet in Victorian design was to let the house speak for itself and not hide the front behind an overwhelming mass of hardscaping or plantings. If you live in an old house, or a well-built new one, chances are that a considerable amount of effort and energy was invested by the architect and builder to make the front of the structure attractive. Why hide all this work? The Victorian ideal was to let the house stand on its own with the foundation "dressed," not buried, in a light planting of mixed flowers and shrubs. The key here is to maintain an ap-

propriate sense of scale, and not plant material near the house that will grow to overwhelm it.

Take a look at the front of Point Ellice House. Notice that while some of the plantings are quite large, none tower over the house and hide it. Many of the plantings are in fact deciduous, which makes them considerably less visually heavy when out of leaf, and also yields the added benefit of providing flowers and fragrance. Plants like roses, lilac, winter jasmine, hardy fuchsias, honeysuckles, and the spectacular *Fremontodendron californicum* all feature prominently. It's significant that

Left: Potted azaleas now stand where Caroline once kept flowering annuals to add color around the entrance of her home. The dowels and brackets, seen to the right of the door, were replicated in 1989 and reveal a clever method the O'Reillys used for supporting climbing plants against the house. Netting was stretched between the dowels so that plants such as sweet peas could climb and add color and scent to the doorway throughout the summer. How much more pleasant a custom than the modern habit of hiding the house behind dreary evergreens!

Right: Considered by the Victorians as "draperies" for the garden, vines were a common feature in period foundation plantings. Here the original white jasmine planted in the 1880s climbs a trellis that was meticulously researched and replicated during the garden's restoration in 1989.

Taken in the 1920s, this photograph clearly shows the overgrowth of ivy and other plantings that began to take over after the turn of the last century. Plantings were later restored to their original Victorian dimensions and scale by the curators in the 1980s.

then as now, the majority of the evergreens are actually very large plants; planted too close, they will very quickly outgrow their intended space and overwhelm the scale of the structure. On a subconscious level, humans prefer light and airy situations and are uncomfortable with plantings that are overly massive and constricting. It's as if our primordial fears of the dangers lurking in the dark, dense forest once again come to the fore. There is also another important consideration: maintenance. The only way to prevent large evergreens like yews, which are really trees, from quickly enveloping a house is to prune massively and often, which is a long, tedious process that can quickly get out of hand if let go.

a number of these plants are climbing vines. Considered the "draperies of the garden" by the Victorians, vines were used extensively by the O'Reillys in the foundation planting, supported on the walls of the house by an ingenious peg-and-string trellising method.

Another important aspect of the O'Reilly garden, and of Victorian gardens in general, is that massive evergreens by and large were kept away from the house structure. Where they do exist, they are held in check by pruning. In general, heavy use of evergreens near a house was frowned upon, because,

In fact, this was exactly what happened at Point Ellice. When the garden was turned over to the Province of British Columbia in the 1970s, there were many large plantings, added during the 1950s and 1960s that had been inappropriately chosen and placed, with the result that they had begun to overwhelm the house and garden. Even well-sited

PETER TO CAROLINE—YALE 5 APRIL 1872

Mashell ought to pull the weeds out of the Croquet ground very carefully so as not to injure the young grass, after rain is the best time, and it should be watered after being weeded, with the liquid manure mixed with water. I hope the rose bushes reached you in safety and that they were planted immediately and well watered. Of course you make them save all the slops and bath water.

historic plantings, like the big hollies on the front lawn, had not been properly pruned in decades and had grown far too large for the intended design. The solution was twofold. First, the nonhistoric material was removed and replaced with more appropriate period choices. Secondly, the historic plants were the subject of a long, involved process of pruning them back to scale over several years. Undertaken in the 1980s, this procedure required a vast amount of effort, expertise, and expense. For the average homeowner, it's far better to avoid using large evergreens near the house in the first place and to concentrate instead on dwarf varieties, as well as suitably sized deciduous materials.

The use of flowers, both perennial and annual, as part of the foundation planting, is also a prominent element of the Point Ellice House garden. In fact throughout the grounds, starting in the early spring, numerous flowers appear to enliven the

landscape. Trying to disguise or hide a foundation with interesing plantings is a far cry from the boring modern scene we so often see around our homes today.

The Grass Was Always Greener

To secure a good lawn, good soil is as essential as for the kitchen garden.

—FRANK SCOTT,
Suburban Home Grounds

A hundred and twenty years ago, the grass *was* in fact greener than it is in many of today's lawns, except of course those bathed in petrochemicals, simply because the Victorians paid attention to something we often forget—the soil beneath our grass. Unlike modern lawns, which are often sown on an inch or two of dirt, lawn preparation in the 1800s was a far more thorough affair involving the creation of a deep soil bed. This process had the advantage of allowing a lawn to root deeply. In times of drought or stress, such lawns could draw upon moisture and nutrients buried in the soil to sustain themselves. Modern lawns, in contrast, either simply brown out or succumb to disease when conditions are too challenging, or else require constant watering and fertilization to stay alive. Although the process of preparing a good soil bed was indeed laborious, the work was

Left: Hardy fuchsias, a favorite plant of the O'Reillys, attract hummingbirds on warm summer days.

Above, right: Hydrangeas in bloom grace the south garden. Unlike our modern reliance on evergreens, the Victorians preferred mixed plantings of deciduous materials for use around the foundation.

THE IMPORTANCE OF EDGING

It would be difficult to place too much emphasis on the role of edging in Victorian gardens like Point Ellice. In the same way that no man would be seen in public without his hat or a woman without a corset, no Victorian drive or path worth its name failed to be constrained and neatly bordered in some way. It is this practice that gives the visual crispness and clarity we so appreciate in these gardens today. At Point Ellice House, the drive as well as the paths are carefully edged either with naturally rounded river stones, or bordered with ivy. Both were carefully installed under the supervision of Peter O'Reilly, who made sure that the margins in his garden were crisp and clear and remained so.

Today, the use of edgings has fallen by the wayside. This is truly a mistake, because a clearly defined border can mean the difference between visual clarity and chaos in the garden. Certainly any garden that aims at historical authenticity needs to pay close attention to edgings. A wide variety of different materials are available as edgers. Which one you use depends on what is common to your area, and what goes best with the other materials already in your yard. Kemp in *How to Lay Out a Small Garden* goes into some detail:

Edgings for walks may be exceedingly various, but there are few indeed that will give lasting satisfaction. Grass is almost the only one that can be altogether commended for pleasure gardens, if well-laid and diligently kept. . . . It furnishes likewise the best ground tint for setting off the colors of flowers, as in a flower garden. It must not be too narrow or it will be difficult to keep cut and the sides will be likely to crumble away.

He continues with a review of other possibilities:

Box edgings are troublesome, liable to great irregularities, apt to harbor insects, not hardy in most parts of the United States, and suitable merely for quaint figures and old fashioned geometrical designs. . . . Rough stones, bricks, thick slates and tiles may make strong and durable edgings for kitchen gardens. The smaller periwinkle, kept in due limits, is useful as an edging under trees; as is the English ivy. The most valuable requisites in an edging are evenness, diminutiveness or capability of being regularly trimmed, quietness in appearance or harmony with whatever is behind it, and permanence. As a rule, all sorts of freak things are to be eschewed, as for example, the wire edgings in vogue some years ago, or edgings of whitewashed stones, or of bricks standing uncertainly on their corners. One occasionally sees flower beds . . . edged with beer bottles, or other convenient debris, which no matter how curious and striking can hardly be said to be ornamental or in good taste.

The croquet lawn basks in the sunlight of a summer afternoon. Notice the carefully placed "cobbles," or river stones, that Peter O'Reilly used to edge his garden beds and paths. These edgings were meticulously restored during the 1980s.

well recompensed by the elimination of the need for the costly, continual watering and fertilizing so often found today.

Experts of the period like Scott and Parsons recommended that before grass was planted, the soil bed should be cultivated to a depth of at least *a foot and a half.* All existing weeds, rocks, stones, and other debris were to be carefully removed, and the soil bed amply enhanced with rotted manure. When this was completed, the bed was to be thoroughly watered, compacted with a roller, and left to rest for several weeks. Any weeds that appeared were assiduously removed. Just before sowing, the ground was to be lightly raked and any last debris taken away. After scattering the seed, the soil was firmed by rolling in both directions, then watered.

Victorian lawns also differed in another way from today's: They were not monocultures. In fact, grass seed mixtures did not usually consist of just fine lawn grass. Many of the coarser meadow grasses were also included, as well as plants today considered weeds, such as clover and dandelion. While this had the effect of giving the lawn a slightly coarse appearance, it also allowed the lawn to stay green far longer in times of drought since plants like clover hold their color even when water stressed. In addition to regular mowing, Victorian lawns were also rolled several times a month, especially during or after a light rain. This

A good lawn roller was essential for producing the flat garden surfaces so prized by the Victorians, and this is the original one used at Point Ellice for lawn, garden pathway, and carriage drive maintenance. The roller was purchased and manufactured locally at Albion Iron Works Ltd., a company in which Peter was shareholder, and appears in many period photos of the house. Incredibly, it is still serviceable today.

practice, which has fallen completely out of fashion today, was really what was responsible for the marvelously flat greenswards so often associated with the period.

For advice on building gravel walks and drives, see pages 110–12 in the appendix.

One of the rarest plants at Point Ellice, and one of the most interesting, both for itself and because of its namesake, is the Fremontia. (Now named *Fremontodendron californicum*, although formerly and still occasionally *Chiranthodendron californicum* or *Fremontia californica*.)

This 6-foot evergreen shrub with hairy stems grows to the left of the front door and is valued for its large 2- to 4-inch yelloworange flowers that make a truly spectacular show when they appear in early summer. Introduced into cultivation in 1855, this California native was reportedly first discovered by the great explorer, topographer, soldier, and statesman John Charles Frémont, who was himself one of the most interesting plant collectors of the Victorian era.

Frémont's story is one of those fascinating tales of self-made men so typical of nineteenth-century America. Born in Charleston, South Carolina, Frémont began his career as a teacher of mathematics for the U.S. Navy. Declining a promotion, he chose instead in 1833 to join an expedition sponsored by the War Department to survey the upper Mississippi and Missouri rivers. During these travels, he learned the science of surveying and mapmaking as well as how to survive in the wilderness. This became his true métier, and Frémont subsequently went on to lead several of his own expeditions in the early 1840s, one of which charted the Oregon Trail and opened a new route to California through the Sierra Nevadas. During all of his expeditions, he collected botanical samples widely, and it was supposedly during one of these early expeditions that he found and brought back a specimen of what would soon be called Fremontia, along with a related species, *Carpenteria californica*. Frémont published accounts of his experiences and travels, which in a collaboration exceedingly rare for the time, were dictated to, then written and edited by his wife, Jessie (the daughter of a Missouri senator whom Frémont had somehow found time to woo and marry, despite her father's objections). His accounts became best-sellers, and Frémont grew quite famous.

Frémont's adventures, however, were just beginning. In 1845, he again set out for California, which at the time still belonged to Mexico, with a surveying party of sixty men

FREMONTIA

whom Frémont had secret instructions to utilize as a military force should a muchanticipated war with Mexico break out. The expected hostilities did in fact erupt, and Frémont was instrumental in setting the stage for California's separation from Mexico and its eventual admission to the Union—all this despite a politically motivated contretemps that resulted in his court-martial. Although he was eventually pardoned by President Polk, he resigned his commission from the army in disgust, and decided to settle in California.

His arrival in California couldn't have been more propitious. In 1849 the gold rush began, and Frémont had previously acquired a substantial ranch near San Francisco. Sure enough, gold was discovered on his property, and Frémont and his wife became fantastically rich. Selected to be one of California's first two senators, he served one term, and was sought out to become the Democratic candidate for president in 1856, on the proviso that he moderate his sharp antislavery views. He refused, and James Buchanan was nominated in his place. Approached by the Republicans, Frémont became their candidate instead, eventually losing to Buchanan in a bitterly fought campaign.

With the outbreak of the Civil War, Frémont was appointed a major general by Lincoln and served in several capacities. His efforts for the Union, however, meant neglecting his mining operations, and unscrupulous business partners managed to swindle away most of his $10 million fortune. Bad business investments did the rest, and by 1870, Frémont was bankrupt. Supported by his wife's literary efforts, and by a brief stint as territorial governor of Arizona, Frémont died in 1890, only a few months after Congress had awarded him a pension that would have given him a modicum of financial security.

Like its namesake, Fremontia has a rather uncompromising nature. Hardy only to –10°C, Fremontia requires a light, welldrained soil in full sun in a position sheltered from cold, drying winds. Rather short-lived (under 20 years), Fremontia is also subject to sudden collapse and death if exposed to excessive cold or wet. Fremontia tolerates light shade and actually prefers a rather poor soil for best growth. A word of caution—the hair on the stems fall off easily during pruning and can sometimes become a severe irritant to the throat and eyes. The use of goggles and a dust mask is advisable—not a terribly high price to pay to own a unique piece of American horticultural history.

CHAPTER III

THE VICTORIAN FLOWER GARDEN

The Blossom Wars • The Cutting Garden • Black Soil and Other Noisome and Laborious Considerations

The Secret of the Victorian Flower Garden: Starting Your Own Seeds

Growing Flowering Annuals • Help in the Garden • PLANTS WITH A PAST: Dahlias

The Blossom Wars

In the nineteenth century, garden styles, as with many other aspects of popular culture, followed distinct trends. This was especially true for flowers, probably the most hallowed element of the Victorian garden, which became the subject of one of the most radical swings in garden fashion ever witnessed.

Before the eighteenth century, both in Europe and America, the floral palette had been rather sedate. Based mostly on perennials and a few ancient annuals, flower gardens had a tendency to peak in the late spring, and then lapse into a peaceful somnolence for the rest of the season. This all changed abruptly with the arrival of a host of new and interesting plants. Most of the annuals, in fact, that we now associate with the summer garden, such as petunias, zinnias, impatiens, and the like were brought back to European and American gardens by specifically organized plant expeditions. These flowers, which essentially extended the floral season throughout the summer and into the fall, were instant hits. It's hard to underestimate the effect of these novelties on the gardening world. Suddenly, gardens could be filled with color from earliest spring till frost, a fact not lost on a culture in love with all

> The pleasure derived from a fine collection of flowers requires no comment, only that the more varied and perpetual the flowering, the greater is the gratification to the observer. The moral lesson that can be obtained from flowers also forms another fine characteristic in the flower garden; for flowers not only please the eye and gratify the passing observer, but contain a beauty in their structure, in the most minute parts and coloring, that conveys a pleasing and natural lesson to the most accurate and intelligent observer, with everything to please, and nothing to offend.
>
> —JOSEPH BRECK,
> *The Flower Garden*

things new and exotic. Coupled with this were the technological advances that by the 1860s allowed professional greenhouses to produce these new species affordably. Seed catalogues and nurseries began actively promoting the use of bright annuals, giving rise to a gardening style known as bedding out.

Bedding out, simply defined, was the practice of using colored annuals in a flower bed to create a pattern, akin to the displays still occasionally seen, and now generally greeted by derisive yawns, in various parks and botanical gardens today. Often created as islands in the lawn, these beds typically featured annuals with flowers and/or variegated foliage, tightly grouped in swirling patterns of color. "Ribbon" beds, with their parallel lines of brilliant, contrasting colors, were planted along walks and paths as edging. In public parks and on estates large-scale "carpet" beds mimicked the richly patterned Oriental rugs, needlepoint, and wall coverings popular in many Victorian homes. Compared to these boldly colored novelties, old-fashioned perennial borders seemed entirely passé, and most of these gardens were soon replanted with colorful annuals.

There were, of course, downsides to this new horticultural fashion—principal among them being the cost. To look their best, these beds had to be replanted twice or three times a year, thus requiring huge numbers of mature, flowering plants for each seasonal show. Maintenance was also a major concern. Before the advent of the ever-blooming varieties

we have today, annuals needed to be actively deadheaded to stay in flower, requiring something of a trapeze act on the part of the gardener to remove faded blooms without crushing the tightly planted displays. Finally, there was the issue of taste. Carpet bedding was easy to do badly, and as more and more people took up the practice, inevitably quite a number of truly ghastly floral combinations began to appear in gardens across Europe and America. It was enough to make the horticultural purist howl, and by the 1870s, the excessive artificiality of this style had started to draw protests.

One rebel was William Robinson, a self-taught plantsman and garden writer. Beginning with his book *The Wild Garden*, 1870, Robinson led the revolt against the bedding-out craze, which he compared to "the cramming of Chinese feet into

Re-created by Point Ellice curators in the 1980s, this heart-shaped bed of roses was the only instance of patterned flower beds at the house.

Point Ellice Flowers

This two-page collection of richly textured floral views from spring and summer illustrate how important flowers were not only to the O'Reillys but also to the Victorian in general.

impossible shoes." Written with a vehement passion in which he waged virtual war against bedding out, Robinson urged readers to "cease the dreadful practice of tearing up the flower-beds and leaving them like new dug graves twice a year" and instead take their cue from nature, using a mixture of annuals, perennials, shrubs, vines, and trees in a loose, informal way.

Robinson's notions of the wild garden influenced many, among them his friend and fellow garden designer Gertrude Jekyll. "I am strongly for treating garden and wooded ground in a pictorial way, mainly with large effects," she wrote in *Wood and Garden*, 1899. "And for so arranging plants and trees and grassy spaces that they look happy and at home, and make no parade of conscious effort."

Trained as an artist, Jekyll saw gardening as "painting a picture with living plants." Her signature style was long perennial borders filled with large drifts of flowers. She urged readers not to be swayed by the "petty tyrannies of the 'florist'" but to keep an open mind as to which plants to use.

For whatever reason, Caroline and Peter never seemed to care much for the bedding-out style. There wasn't a single annual carpet bed at Point

Lilies of all colors and varieties (like this golden type, perhaps the long-thought-lost *H. flava*) were grown by the O'Reillys and often sent to friends as gifts.

Ellice, although the practice was indeed known and actively pursued in other gardens around Victoria. Instead, they built flower beds throughout the garden that contained an informal mix of both annuals and perennials. Nor, with one exception (the heart-shaped rose garden), did they follow the contemporary practice of cutting artificially shaped beds out of the lawn. At Point Ellice, softly curving beds of flowers nestle naturally along pathways backed by shrub roses and other blossoming shrubs, tuck themselves into the foundation planting amid ivy and holly, or swirl down the drive fronted by cobbles. Flowers are everywhere at Point Ellice: They intertwine and weave themselves into the general landscape, blurring the distinction between flower bed, border, and general landscape.

Remarkably, Caroline and Peter's naturalistic tendencies did not reflect the shifting trends in gardening, but foreshadowed them. By the time Robinson's first anti-artificial manifesto appeared in 1870, the O'Reillys were well on their way to planning, and planting, their garden. By the time Jekyll called for releasing flower borders from the "crudest and most garish effects" of the formal bedding system, the natura-

PETER TO CAROLINE—30 APRIL 1876

I am glad you have had the trees planted; you have not I hope, forgotten to put in a lot of the young bloom trees and be sure to have the seeds sown in the garden soon, after an abundant supply of manure has been dug in.

listic design of the Point Ellice gardens was already decades old. *For advice on naturalizing bulbs, see page 128 in the appendix.*

The Cutting Garden

There was, however, one area of the garden that was dedicated almost exclusively to flowers. As the city of Victoria became more established and the O'Reillys' need for growing a large portion of their own produce lessened, somewhere along the line the south kitchen garden began to acquire more and more flowers, until by the turn of the century, a considerable section had been transformed into a cutting garden. Period photos of Kathleen show her watering there, amidst a field of flowers that would be the envy of any gardener today. How did she achieve such lush effects? The answer lay in the soil.

Black Soil and Other Noisome and Laborious Considerations

The process of building up one's soil was a very different affair 135 years ago, and certainly didn't involve a trip to the hardware store to rent a roto-tiller and grab a bag of 10-10-10. (Neither chemical fertilizers nor mechanical cultivators became common until after World War II.) In the Victorian era, good gardening both for flowers and for vegetables meant two things, trenching and manure—lots of it.

While the term sounds fairly innocuous, trenching was in fact quite the contrary. It was a fantastically laborious process that involved digging a long trench the width of the garden bed 2 feet deep and placing the soil aside in barrows. Next, another trench was dug beside the first, and the soil from the second replaced the first, and so on and so on until the last trench was reached and filled with the soil still in the barrows from the initial digging. Trenching had the advantage of mixing together the contents in the subsoil and the topsoil, producing a deep, easily drained, rich bed. Manure was often added at the same time to enrich the mix further. Unfortunately for many gardeners, this method presumed that the topsoil in question was at

Kathleen watering the kitchen/cutting garden in the summer of 1902. Watering with a hose from town water, instead of using a bucket from the well, was a novelty much welcomed by the Victorians.

least a foot deep. Anything less would result in too much subsoil being brought to the surface. In such cases, a process called bastard trenching was used. The topsoil was removed and transferred as above, but the subsoil in each trench stayed in place and was decompacted with a pick; several inches of fresh manure were then added above it, which would help to amend the upper subsoil and provide a greater depth of topsoil for subsequent trenchings.

Manure was the key ingredient in Victorian gardens and there was plenty of it to be had not only from the farmyard, but also from chamber pots. In fact, the Victorian world was full of it. The average single horse, like Kathleen O'Reilly's favorite, Blackie, produced over twelve thousand pounds of the stuff each year. Add to this all the manure produced by the other farm animals, plus the daily contents of the chamber pots (euphemistically called black soil and much prized for horticultural use), and the average household had one large odiferous problem. The solution, of course, lay in the garden, which received the lion's share of this bounty. Tons and tons were rotted in piles and pits and then dug into the flower beds, vegetable plots, even diluted with water and poured on the lawn. At Point Ellice, this rather unpleasant duty was left to Chinese servants who helped with the garden.

All this manure had another benefit. Unlike modern chemical fertilizers that contain only nutrients, manure also improved the consistency and drainage of the soil. Rather surprisingly, the Victorians weren't in the least squeamish about the whole affair, and in fact conducted heated debates as to which manure was best. Shirley Hibberd's *Profitable Gardening*, 1863, proposes one hierarchy:

> If a given quantity of land, sown without manure yields three times the seed employed, the same quantity of land will produce five times the quantity sown when manured with old herbage, putrid grass or leaves, garden stuff, etc; seven times with cow-dung, nine times with pigeon dung; ten times with horse dung; twelve times with human urine; twelve times with goat dung; twelve times with sheep-dung; and fourteen times with human manure. . . .

CAROLINE TO PETER—14 MAY 1871

I did not go out on Friday except to garden—the weeds are dreadful—it is a never-ending labor. The little man [Frank] works away like a Trojan and the Puss-pie [Kathleen] runs about doing nothing. The Pop [Mary Augusta] runs about too—she does not like to sit in her carriage and of course when she is running about she is always in trouble about picking the flowers . . .

If all this talk of trenching and manure seems to leave the modern gardener in a bit of a fix, it does. After all, unless you happen to keep a few horses around, it's hard to come by animal manure in such quantities. Human manure of course has long since been banned from the garden for health reasons. The answer to this dilemma actually lies in the above quote "old herbage, putrid grass or leaves," which we otherwise know today as compost. While not as strong as animal manures, compost packs quite a punch in terms of soil improvement, and anyone really interested in duplicating the luxuriant feel of the Victorian garden would be wise to become a master of the composting process—a simple feat to do given the number of excellent easy-to-follow guides now available. As for trenching, to be honest, it is indeed a laborious, back-twisting process, but unfortunately no amount of rototilling will ever compare to the thorough mixing of texture and nutrients such a digging over provides.

As a test several years ago we prepared two identical plots for flowers and vegetables, one trenched, the other rototilled. The results were dramatic. The trenched side produced far more—almost double—the quantity of blooms and produce under identical growing conditions. So much for modern improvements. The only solace we can offer is that if you decide to undertake this trench-

These English publications dating from 1908 to 1909 provide detailed information on growing orchids and chrysanthemums (both then all the rage) as well as tender bedding plants. Kathleen's love of gardening, acquired when she was a girl, remained with her all her life. An avid amateur gardener, she frequently entered flowers from Point Ellice House in flower shows sponsored by the Victoria Horticultural Society and repeatedly took first and second prize.

ing process in your garden, the results will be astonishing, and unless your soil is very poor, it only needs to be done once a decade or so. The other years the garden can simply receive a topdressing of manure or compost, which can then be lightly dug or tilled in. Small comfort, but better than none.

The Secret of the Victorian Flower Garden: Starting Your Own Seeds

After proper soil preparation, what separates Victorian flower gardens from modern examples is their uniqueness. In the 1800s, nurseries were found in only the most urban areas, and most people, like the O'Reillys, ordered seeds from an almost endless selection available from a host of mail order catalogues. Conceived and grown by the gardeners themselves, flower gardens of that era were thus completely personal and individual. This was certainly the case at Point Ellice, where perusing seed catalogues and marking the next season's selections was one of the O'Reillys' most prized family activities.

If you want this same wonderful Victorian variety in your flower garden, you need to do a bit of catalogue homework and start your own plants. You can't get the interesting combinations of

From left to right: Dame's rocket and foxglove, as well as white lilac, grace the spring garden. The original O'Reilly hollyhocks blooming in the north garden, with woodland forming a protective background. If you want rare plants like these in your garden, you will have to start them from seeds.

shape and color found in a Victorian garden by trooping down to the local nusery and buying whatever happens to be on hand. The inevitable result will be a cookie-cutter selection of flowers that matches your neighbor's and their neighbors' and theirs. Instead, spend a little time perusing the many wonderful catalogues that list unique selections, especially those with period and heirloom flowers. These colorful issues usually arrive in early January and February, just when the weather is at its dreariest and you need them the most. What could be more delightful than sitting with your feet up by a cozy fire dreaming about the spectacular things that will be growing in your garden the next season?

There's another very good reason to consider starting your own plants—cost. Even the most mathematically challenged can figure out that with tiny plant six-packs currently priced at anywhere between $2.00 and $4.00, a packet of seeds that costs $1.50 and produces fifty plants is a much bet-

ter deal, even when you factor in the cost of the soil, flats, and assorted other equipment required for the job.

One important caveat, however: Garden catalogues are highly addictive, so you'll often end up ordering far more than you really need. Instead, keep a firm hand and start small. While growing your own plants isn't difficult, it does take some time and effort. It's best not to overwhelm yourself on your first attempt and become discouraged. One of the best ways to begin is to start with annuals. Annuals are easy to grow, produce quick results, and are a great way to gather experience for the slightly more demanding process of growing biennials and perennials.

Growing Flowering Annuals

Annuals are generally divided into two groups: the so-called hardy varieties that can be planted outside directly into the ground, and the "half hardy" types that need to be started earlier indoors. Sunflowers and zinnias, for instance, are hardy annuals, requiring a much shorter season to bloom. They can and should be planted directly into the garden. Plants like petunias, on the other hand, which need a very long growing season to flower, should be started indoors. The directions on each packet will tell you which category the plant belongs to. The first thing to do when your seed order arrives is to separate the packets into two groups for indoor and outdoor planting. If you are planning to grow many different varieties, you may also find it helpful to make a chart showing what needs to be planted when and where. Once you get the seeds arranged, place the packets in an airtight container in the freezer until you are ready to use them. Seeds can last a remarkably long time, years, in fact, when properly stored, and if you want good germination, it's important to keep them away from warmth and moisture until you are ready to plant.

Snapdragons border the path along the croquet lawn.

There is no great trick to planting hardy annuals directly into the garden. Just follow the directions on the packet. For some reason, however, people these days are hesitant to do so, preferring instead to start seeds indoors even when not required. It's almost as if in this age of instant everything we lack the faith that the seeds will even sprout when left to their own devices in the great outdoors. The leap of faith required, however, will be more than justified when you see the delightful results that follow. The O'Reillys always planted many of their annuals directly in the ground, and you should too. In fact, this is another one of the secrets to the charming randomness found in a Victorian garden. The seeds inevitably shift about in the soil, helped by squirrels and other such creatures, and plants will often appear where least expected. You will also discover that those varieties that can be planted directly outside actually prefer it, and will perform better than the same plants started inside and transplanted outside later.

Half-hardy annuals require a bit more coddling. The first step in the process is to get things organized. You'll need a long table or bench in an area like a greenhouse, basement, or garage, where you won't mind spilling a bit of dirt on the floor. This is more than likely one of the reasons the O'Reillys eventually built their own small greenhouse. You'll also need access to water. A hose is really best, but a sprinkling can will do. Use plastic seed-starter trays, called flats, with clear plastic lids, which are available at most garden shops and from seed catalogues. And of course you'll need some soil. Although technically you could use garden soil (the Victorians certainly did), it is generally best to use what's called a soilless mix, so named because it technically doesn't contain soil at all. This special creation is a mixture of peat moss and vermiculite, and has the advantage of retaining moisture, as well as being sterile. Young seedlings are particularly susceptible to a fungal disease called dampening off, which causes the little stems to rot away at the base. Using a sterile mixture can often avoid this problem.

When sowing seeds, always place the soil in the flat and water it heavily *before* seeding. Although this seems a bit odd, this method not only allows the soil to settle in the container, preventing air pockets, but also assures that you won't wash away your precious seeds with an overzealous initial watering.

Once you have prepared your containers, watered them, and allowed them to drain, you are ready to proceed with the seeding. Sowing large seeds is easy. You just press them into the soil until they are covered. Although the rule varies from variety to variety, in general, seeds should be buried about twice the measurement of their length. For most seeds, this isn't very deep, and it's best to err on the side of shallow planting. Planting too deeply is one of the leading causes of poor germination. Extremely small seeds can simply be scattered over the soil surface and pressed in with

your hand or a wooden block. When you're done, cover the flats with their clear plastic lids, or a bit of plastic wrap to keep in the moisture. Place the flats in a warm, sunny space or under fluorescent light in the basement, which works very well as long as the flats are kept no more than 4 inches from the bulb. Water gently when the soil begins to dry. If you keep the flats covered, this may take a week or more. Remove the lids from the flats when the young seedlings are an inch or two high, watering only when required.

Surprisingly, the most important factor in getting seeds to germinate is not light, as most people assume, but soil temperature. Most annual seeds need a fairly warm, constant soil temperature, 70°F or so, in order to germinate regularly. This is one of nature's built-in safety mechanisms to prevent the seed from sprouting before the outside temperatures have risen high enough to support the plant. The Victorians knew this, and often placed flats of seeds on tops of beds of rotting manure, called hot frames, where the heat from the decomposition would warm the flats. Given the fact that your stables may be a bit empty these days, one of the best ways for assuring good germination temperatures is to use one of the special heating cables found at any nursery or garden

PETER TO CAROLINE—1 MAY 1870

In selecting the garden seeds don't forget sweet pea, scarlet runner, mignonette and such like, but you know much better than I do … [Mashell] ought to draw a good pile of gravel and also of black soil, if not useful this year it will be useful next when we may not have the means of getting it … the black soil ought to be piled outside near the manure heap. Tell John to have the manure well covered up.

shop. These little devices are like little electric blankets that sit under the flats, keeping the soil and the seeds at a constant, cozy temperature.

Once your seeds have sprouted, they should be acclimatized to the outdoors in the cold frame. Then they are finally ready for planting outdoors. If your plants were grown for a general border, they may be simply placed in their intended spots, making sure to keep in mind their ultimate height and spacing requirements. Smaller, shorter plants always go toward the front, with larger and progressively taller specimens toward the rear.

Flowers intended principally for cutting, however, are best grown in a separate cutting garden as they were at Point Ellice. Planted in rows similar to a vegetable garden, this arrangement had the dual benefit of preserving the floral display in the borders, while making the harvesting of flowers for use inside the house far easier to do—which just happens to be the subject of the next chapter.

For information on cold frames and hot beds, as well as how to build your own cold frame, see pages 113–14 in the appendix.

PETER TO CAROLINE—25 APRIL 1872

By tomorrow's boats I will send you the rose bushes and a splendid sweet briar from the Hudson Bay garden—say nothing of it—but I think I would for this summer plant all in the shade near the Drakes garden and then water well. Be sure to send Mashell to the steamer at once and plant the same evening. I also send a few lilacs.

CAROLINE TO PETER—8 MAY 1871

I did not go out to drive on Friday but spent the day with the children in the garden thinking constantly of you and of how constantly you laboured to leave it all in order for us. The place is looking very pretty—the grass has been cut all over and is springing again. The stocks and the wall flowers are in beautiful bloom and the laurestinus in front of our bedroom window has at last come out and looks lovely now—how I wish you could see it! The roses I got from Mitchell are not very successful: they will not bloom this year and I fear it was too late, I suppose, to transplant them.

HELP IN THE GARDEN

CAROLINE TO PETER—10 MAY 1873

I sent Joseph to borrow the machine from Mrs. Jenns and he has cut the croquet lawn and now he says he does not want to stay, that he has heard of a place that suits him better…of course it is a worry and anxiety to have to look for someone else and to have to tell them the same thing over again.

CAROLINE TO PETER—18 MAY 1873

At last we have succeeded in getting a man who I believe to be steady and a worker. His name is Will McColl…The man appears to be going on satisfactorily. He has cleaned the fowl house well and has put in some cauliflower plants, sticked the peas, thoroughly cleaned the garden path, and today he has cut the grass on the point. It is so long that he has left it to make hay for the cow….

CAROLINE TO PETER—8 APRIL 1875

Old Fung bustled out and planted the ivy. I think he has done it well. Charley cleaned the harness and the carriage and worked in the garden. Fredrike came back from town in a very bad temper and was very impertinent….I was greatly tempted to tell her that she must seek another place, but I restrained myself….Tuesday evening I devoted to writing.

In the days before automated machinery made domestic work so much less time consuming, maintaining a house and garden, even a modest one like Point Ellice, required a staff. Finding, supervising, and keeping good help was a never-ending task, one that was pretty much left to Caroline. In general, the O'Reillys usually retained one female servant, who served as a nursemaid and did general housework and cleaning. They also employed at least one Chinese houseboy (generally referred to by Peter in those nonpolitically correct days as "the Chinaman"), who helped with the cooking, did some of the heavier household chores such as cleaning fireplaces and keeping the kitchen range burning as well as light labor outdoors, such as weeding the kitchen garden or rolling the lawn. Both the maid and the houseboy lived at Point Ellice. In addition, there was generally a part-time gardener and a laundress who appeared weekly, as well as a whole list of service personnel, including dressmakers, carpenters, painters, and piano tuners who came as needed. Here are some of the names you will encounter in the O'Reilly letters from the 1860s, 1870s, and 1880s:

Female Servants	*Chinese Servants*	*Gardeners*	*Carpenters*
Rose McGlone	Fung	"Old" James	*(who frequently worked on the house for Peter)*
Lizzie Deasy	Tom	William Crogan	
Lena Burgess	Charley	J. Clayton	Eli Harrison
Fanny Bickford	Se-You	Robert Newall	A. W. Davey
Elizabeth Strathorn	Sing	George Elvin	
Ellen Crogan	Song	William Clarke	*Dressmakers*
Louisa	Goon	A. Ohlsen	*(for Caroline and Kathleen)*
	Hick		Mrs. Williamson *(the local dressmaker)*
	Chin		Sarah Scotter *(in England, who made a lot of evening dresses for both ladies)*
	Quong		

Hurrah! . . . it is a frost! The dahlias are all dead!

—ROBERT SMITH SURTEES,
Handley Cross

While it's dubious that the O'Reillys would have shared this view of dahlias (they featured prominently in the Point Ellice House gardens a hundred years ago and are very much part of the restored garden today), it is true that the dahlia has been something of a garden misfit since it first departed the New World for the Old.

Beloved by the Aztecs as a medicinal plant, the dahlia left its native Mexico for the Royal Gardens at Madrid in 1789, imported not for its flowers, which in the original species are a rather simple yellow, but because it was believed its fleshy tuber might make a new and useful vegetable. Judged "edible, but not agreeable," the tubers never made it to the table. But the "brilliant, barbaric flowers" (to quote plant historian Alice Coats) of *Dahlia pinnata* did manage to attract the attention of various European hybridizers, who thought the six-foot-high plant held promise as an exotic annual. Crosses were made in France and Spain, and Empress Josephine planted some of the first in her garden at Malmaison. Several of these varieties were imported to England after the Napoleonic Wars, where by 1830, they had become all the rage. *D. pinnata* was rapidly transformed through crossbreeding from a fairly simple, large, flowering plant into a plethora of different varieties in all sizes, shapes, and colors.

The dahlia's newfound popularity did not come without controversy, however. Considered by many to be garish, as early as 1823 English nurseryman Thomas Hogg considered them "too large for the small flower garden" and "best adapted to fill up the vacancies in the ornamental shrubberies." Some people felt even that usage too much, and dahlias, whose big, loud flowers are always hard to ignore, were one of the first casualties when garden fashion changed at the turn of the century away from brilliantly

DAHLIAS

colored exotics to a more subdued, perennial palette. Dahlias have always had their ardent admirers, however, and hundreds of new introductions continued to be made over the years. Today, dahlias have regained much of their popularity. Thousands of varieties, including many period ones, exist, divided into eighteen classifications according to flower type, ranging from human-sized plants with 8-inch peony-like flowers, to small single varieties only 6 inches high. These days, there really is a dahlia for almost every garden style and setting.

Dahlia culture is really quite simple. Purchase tubers in the spring, and plant in rich soil, about 6 inches deep. Do pay attention to the growth requirements, however: Dahlias vary wildly in habit, especially the older, taller varieties, and you need to make sure that you choose the right one for your site. After planting and mulching, keep well watered and fertilized—then watch them take off. Dahlias grow quickly and aren't especially troubled by pests. Occasionally diseases such as mosaic virus can be an issue. Quick removal of infected plants generally keeps the problem from spreading.

Although many people treat their dahlias as annuals, they are actually tender perennials, hardy to Zone 10, and particularly nice specimens of historic cultivars are often worth saving. There are many different ways to overwinter dahlias, but here's one of the easiest: Simply cut the plant back to 1 foot above the ground just prior to hard frost, and carefully raise the tubers. Carefully remove any attached dirt (you may need to wash them with a hose), as well as any rotted or injured parts of the tuber. Let dry for a few hours. Prune the stems back to the tubers, label, and place in loose plastic bags, with a few holes punched in for air circulation. Store the tubers just like you would potatoes in a cool, dry place at 35 to 40°F. The O'Reillys most likely overwintered them in the root cellar, but these days the veggie drawer in the refrigerator works just as well. Replant in the garden when all danger of frost is past.

CHAPTER IV
BRINGING THE GARDEN INDOORS

The Outside Moves In • Windows Alive • Kathleen at Court • Gardening Under Glass: Wardian Cases and Greenhouses
Orchids: A Story of Seduction • Arranging Flowers • Dressing for Success
PLANTS WITH A PAST: Scented Geraniums

It was inevitable that a family like the O'Reillys, so in tune with the styles of the times, would follow fashion and work to beautify their outdoor landscape. For a socially conscious Victorian, however, the aesthetic demands of proper horticulture did not stop at the front door. The greenery inside their home was also considered a direct reflection of the inhabitants' taste and character. Luckily, one of the easiest and most fashionable ways to demonstrate this sophistication was through the avid use of indoor plants. Even the humblest worker's cottage could be transformed into a "home of taste" through the display of a few simple flowers. As Shirley Hibberd wrote in his 1895 bible for the period aesthetic, *Rustic Adornments for Homes of Taste,*

> A home without flowers is bare and comfortless to all persons of taste and refinement.
>
> —F. W. BURBIDGE,
> *Domestic Floriculture*

In the adornment of the home, it does not require a princely fortune to set up a vase of flowers . . . and any poor homeowner may everyday experience a subdued but healthy pleasure amidst ferns and flowers: the rose will shake into his heart her perfume, and the lily recall to him the teachings of the Lord.

While this type of didactic piety may have been the gardening goal of the socially concerned, religion was far from the minds of most middle-class gardeners. For them, indoor cultivation of tropical exotics was the means of associating themselves, albeit distantly, with the much-admired greenhouses and conservatories of the aristocracy.

As with other aspects of Victorian household

management, the responsibility for "parlor gardening," as it was often called, fell to the women. At Point Ellice that meant Caroline and Kathleen were in charge, as F. W. Burbidge notes in his 1874 work, *Domestic Horticulture:*

> In tasteful homes, where there are ladies, parlor gardening may safely be left in their hands and it is astonishing what quick progress the dear, nimble-fingered creatures make in this delightful art.

Without the expertise of modern decorators, or the ability to pop off to the local florist, those "nimble-fingered creatures" developed their own art style, inspired by the need to present their houseplants properly. The women of the day crammed crafts projects into their already busy schedules by laboring over such creations as picture frames decorated with bits of pine cones and moss, ferns pressed into papers and lamp shades,

A period parlor arrangement.

arrangements of exotics on stands, and entire miniature landscapes under glass. Through parlor gardening and its companion arts and crafts, the magical world of the garden could be extended into the house.

The Outside Moves In

We always feel welcome when, on entering a room, we find a display of flowers on the table. When there are flowers about, the hostess appears glad, the children pleased, the very dog and cat grateful for our arrival. The whole scene and all the personages seem more hearty, homely, and beautiful.

—SHIRLEY HIBBERD,
*Rustic Adornments
for Homes of Taste*

For most of us today, indoor gardening means potted plants, a half dozen terra-cotta containers on a living-room table or a line of plastic pots

An ivy-draped mirror; the pot, cleverly, is part of the frame, hidden behind the glass.

above the kitchen sink. Our plants may be lovely, perhaps even exotic, but almost inevitably they are relegated to one or two specific places, separate from the television set, the coffee table, or the bedroom dresser. Victorian homemakers and decorators conceived a much more encompassing attitude toward indoor plantings. Just as

Above: While often advocated in period style books, just how common elaborate "parlor bowers" like this one were remains something of a question.

Below: An ivy screen for the drawing room, with flowers at its base.

they tended to think of their gardens as extensions of their homes, Victorians also considered houseplants part of their furniture. Flowers, vines, foliage, and plants in pots were as vital adornments as the furnishings, carpeting, and wall coverings. For many Victorian homes, the lushness inside easily matched the greenery in the garden.

It was a common practice in the Victorian era, and remains a foundation of interior design today, to create a focal point in every room. For Victorians, that centerpiece was very often living. Burbidge recommended using the yucca "with its noble crimson tints" or a ficus or any other "distinct and effective plant" as a way to catch people's eyes when they entered a room. To accent different parts of the room, he advocated growing ivy, "for it grows well in the shade and may be employed for trailing around sofas or couches." A large chair or chaise could be transformed into a bower by sheltering it under an ivy-covered trellis. A unique drawing-room divider could be created by growing a wall of ivy on a frame and edging it with a flower-box base. Even small pictures or mirrors found themselves framed in ivy. For formal occasions, a particularly adept decorator might use palms to adorn their parlor or ferns to adorn a staircase. With collections of plants tucked into the corners and crimson baize covering the floors, the sophisticated scene would be complete.

PETER TO CAROLINE—12 OCTOBER 1877

Learn all you can from Mr. Jenna about saving the roses and geraniums during the winter. Look to your plants if the frost sets in, and be sure the cellar window is closed and the blanket nailed up. And ask the Chinaman each night if he has put the turkeys into the house.

On the walls, where today we would find framed pictures, posters, or even lighting sconces, Victorians again cultivated greenery. Burbidge urged the use of bracket pots and fern bricks as a way for a gardener "to economise the space at his command as much as possible." Ivy, *Lysimachia nummularia*, and other foliage plants flowed from these ornate fixtures, some designed to look like clam shells, mounted on fancy tiles and hung on the wall.

Windows Alive

By growing flowers in our windows we contribute towards the education and refinement of society at large—we make our homes in the town not only happier, but more attractive both to ourselves and our children, and we are often led to form habits of observation and study which ultimately prove of eminent service to us in afterlife.

—F. W. BURBIDGE

When the Victorians talked about gardening in windows, they usually didn't just mean window boxes. While such containers were indeed used, especially on balconies, to the Victorians, window gardening referred more to the staging of plants in an oversized window to create the effect of a miniature landscape inside. Point Ellice is a perfect example. In the course of their extensive home renovations in 1877, the O'Reillys expanded the dining room to include just such a space. The drawing room, too, had a bay window that was later enlarged. In both locations, the family dis-

played an extensive collection of plants arranged on tables and stands.

Part of the attraction window gardening had for the Victorians was that before the nineteenth century, gardening indoors was pretty much an impossibility. In most homes small windows with thick, uneven glass conspired to limit indoor light severely, while primitive heating systems sent rooms from freezing to boiling during the course of a single day. As late as 1864, Edward Sprague Rand, Jr., had to warn the readers of his book, *Flowers for the Parlor and Garden,*

Top: An interior window box.

Above: A window box and aquarium combined—to modern eyes a rather odd juxtaposition.

Left: A large window conservatory.

to "choose a room where the temperature at night never falls below forty to forty-five degrees." In most new homes today, even garages or basements never come close to such cold, but Victorian gardens had to live with such climate extremes indoors on a regular basis.

Another pitfall to successful indoor horticulture was the gas used to light many homes. The slightest whiff of leaked gas, almost inevitable with the turning on and off of fixtures, could cause the plants to droop and leaves to fall. But by the 1870s, advances in heating, ventilation, and lighting began to transform parlors into viable environments for growing tender flowering and foliage plants; and window gardening emerged as part of the larger trend of embellishing the home. Windows, porches, and balconies suddenly seemed unnecessarily empty if they didn't host the requisite arrangements of potted plants.

A Victorian homeowner with a large, south-facing bay window had in essence a readymade solarium. If the window wasn't already deep enough, a shelf was easily fashioned from a 3-foot plank with rounded edges that extended into the room. To the top of this platform was often fitted a wooden box lined with zinc to catch any errant splashes of water or drainage from pots.

An ideal Victorian window garden, complete with a selection of potted floor plants, Wardian case, and hanging pots.

As with everything else Victorian, window gardens ranged from the simply elegant to the elegantly outrageous. Dense windows were often packed with ivy or other climbers that framed bright, bold flowers. The selection of plants was determined by their tolerance of temperature fluctuations. Hardy plants such as camellias were recommended for their resistance to the cold as well as for their outstanding winter flowers. Orange and lemon trees, other plants that prefer cool winter temperatures, were another favorite, though they required more care to thrive. Azaleas were "a strong growing plant . . . [that] may be grown in great perfection" with good drainage and vigilant awareness of the plant's watering needs. Homeowners with widely varying temperatures were warned to stay away from exotics and stick to the basic fuchsias, geraniums, and balsams that will "keep gay through the summer and autumn."

On deep bay windows, glass doors were often employed to shut the plants off from the rest of the room. Isolating them allowed the Victorian grower a bit more control over their environment, protecting

KATHLEEN'S DIARY—11 MARCH 1887

Frightful gale blowing . . . after lunch arranged dinner table with moss and crocuses and picked violets.

KATHLEEN AT COURT

Being presented at court was a ceremony that usually marked a girl's passage into womanhood, although not always, as in the case of Kathleen O'Reilly. At the ripe old age of twenty-nine, she was presented to Lord Lieutenant and Countess Cadogan on February 17, 1897. The event was arranged as an afterthought as she traveled to Britain with her childhood friend Jessie Dunsmuir, later Lady Musgrave, and her husband Sir Richard. The following letter from Kathleen to her parents, dated February 23, 1897, describes the event.

MY DEAR FATHER & MOTHER,

The going up to Dublin was quite an afterthought when I came over here. I telegraphed to Scotter [Sarah Scotter, Kathleen's dressmaker] to send my white ball dress which is covered with sparkles and trimmed with Lilies of the Valley and a train. She sent the latter, white lined with delicate shade of green & trimmed with little lilies and white & green bows of ribbon. It was so very spring looking a girl of seventeen could have worn it. . . .

I was rather nervous about the ordeal of being presented and had so many instructions about curtseying first and then presenting your left cheek for the Lord Lieutenant to kiss. I was told to do it all very slowly as some people get so frightened that they rush past the dais where all the Vice Regal party are standing. I gave my card to the Officer at the Throne Room door

Kathleen in her gown, ready to be presented at Court.

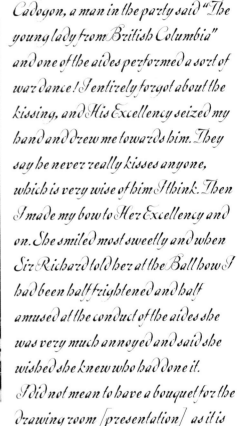

who said "Curtsey first, won't you" in a sort of sympathising tone and then I heard my name simply shouted which was rather disconcerting in itself, but when I got in front of Lord Cadogon, a man in the party said "The young lady from British Columbia" and one of the aides performed a sort of war dance! I entirely forgot about the kissing, and His Excellency seized my hand and drew me towards him. They say he never really kisses anyone, which is very wise of him I think. Then I made my bow to Her Excellency and on. She smiled most sweetly and when Sir Richard told her at the Ball how I had been half frightened and half amused at the conduct of the aides she was very much annoyed and said she wished she knew who had done it.

I did not mean to have a bouquet for the drawing room [presentation] as it is not necessary if one has a fan, and I had the Annie Pooley one, but when I found Effie had ordered one for me with theirs I did not like to say anything. I was sorry as it cost two pound two shillings. And it was very lovely—quite bridal white & green lilies, orchids, roses, and gardenias with maiden hair fern etc. & long trails. I don't know what you will say to all this exporting. . . .

them from rapid temperature changes and leaking gas, especially if some provision was made for keeping the space warm at night. Plant washing was another Victorian habit, a very beneficial one often forgotten today. Rand in *Flowers for the Parlor and Garden* implored:

> This must be done frequently, [since] a plant breathes, like an animal, and not through one mouth, but thousands. . . . Now we are careful in our own persons to bathe daily, lest, as we say, the pores of the skin become obstructed; yet we are willing to allow our plants to go unwashed for a whole winter.

His quaint advice continues on the subject of watering.

> The temperature of the water is of vital importance. It should neither be cold nor warm, but just the temperature of the atmosphere of the room. Thus no check, or chill, or undue excitement is given to the roots. . . .

Proper pots were considered crucial to success with indoor plants. In her 1853 book, *Ladies' Companion to the Flower Garden*, Jane Webb Loudon recommends common red earthenware pots because they are the most porous and consequently do not retain too much moisture, thus preventing root rot. If fancier containers were to

Two Victorian-era containers.

be used, Loudon instructed readers to fill the bottom third of the container with broken crocks or shards to ensure good drainage—a sound piece of advice for growers today. Regarding the window display itself, Loudon advised that pots should not be packed too close together as flowers will compete for sun and result in "pale sickly plants, drawn up to an unnatural length, and so weak that their stems will not stand upright without the aid of a stick."

For advice on planting a Victorian window box and deciding what might go in it, see pages 115–116 in the appendix.

Gardening Under Glass: Wardian Cases and Greenhouses

Though indoor climates somewhat improved during the latter half of the 1800s, the environment could still be hostile. In addition to the drafts, dry heat, and gas leaks, houseplants had to endure pests. In the nineteenth century, there were many crude and sometimes dangerous pesticides available, some of which were applied in a manner guaranteed to poison the gardener as well as the insect. There were also a few early organic remedies. For example, red spiders and aphids were fought using a natural remedy, the

Two Victorian Wardian cases.

Quassia chip, named after an eighteenth-century slave who discovered its medicinal value. Just an ounce of the heartwood from tropical trees in the ailanthus family would be boiled in three pints of water, which could then be sponged onto infested plants.

Many of these indoor-gardening challenges, however, were solved to a certain degree by a physician in the early part of the century. In order to observe the emergence of a sphinx moth, Dr. Nathaniel Ward planted a stick with an attached cocoon in some garden soil at the bottom of a sealed glass container. Like all unsterilized soil, his dirt contained seeds that eventually germinated. As the scientific belief at the time held that plants needed ventilation to survive, Ward believed the seedlings would promptly die off in the supposedly "airless" container. Instead, the greenery flourished. Soon the curious doctor became more interested in the flora than the fauna. He experimented with a variety of plants in containers, which soon became known as Wardian cases, and were the forerunners of today's terrariums.

Wardian cases quickly became popular in the most tasteful and elaborately furnished rooms. Many were designed of iron, copper, or wood. Some were even finished with delicate enamel and gilding. Smaller cases rested on ornamental stands or were placed on tables as decorations. Larger freestanding cases mimicked glass conservatories

KATHLEEN TO PAPA—23 JUNE 1881

We have had much rain lately…but it was of benefit to the garden. You asked in your last letter to Mama if the box for the flowers at the dining room window had been put up. We did it a day or two after we returned from Yale. We now have three tables with plants in the dining room and one in the drawing room, also in the box outside the dining room window and the shelves in the porch. The pear tree in the berry bed near the croquet lawn is in blossom now.

ORCHIDS: A STORY OF SEDUCTION

While Wardian cases were popular with all classes of society, for a long time the grander practice of gardening in glass houses remained the exclusive province of the very wealthy. Greenhouse technology had existed as long ago as ancient Rome—one of the very first was found in the ruins of Pompeii—but the cost and difficulty of making glass, not to mention exceedingly high tariffs many governments placed on the commodity, kept them out of most gardens. Then, in the middle of the century, the repeal of glass taxes, coupled with technological innovations in production, caused prices to plummet. Suddenly greenhouses became not only affordable, but commercially viable. Greenhouse construction methods were standardized, and mechanisms for ventilating and heating hothouses improved. By the 1880s, prefabricated greenhouses began appearing on the market. Middle-class families like the O'Reillys, who had so long associated the glass house with privilege and wealth, lost no time in acquiring their own. Probably constructed in 1898, the Point Ellice greenhouse not only provided a place for the efficient starting of outdoor seedlings, but also allowed the family, at last, to indulge in the latest plant fad—the cultivation of orchids.

In the horticultural world of the 1890s, no plant evoked more prestige than the orchid. With thirty thousand species growing on every continent except Antarctica, the orchid had figured prominently in the art of ancient China and the legends of medieval Europe. But for centuries, western exposure to the truly exotic tropical orchids, the queens of the species, was limited to sea captains and a few hardy explorers.

Europe's first big encounter with these tropical wonders was serendipitous. In 1818, an English horticulturist, William Cattley, received a shipment of plants from overseas. As he unpacked his plants, Cattley found some strange leaves that were used to pro-

Dendrobium phalaenonpsis, from a rare color lithograph in *The Gardener's Assistant*, an important Victorian gardening manual.

tect the imported material. Intrigued, he potted the stems and in November was rewarded when a gorgeous lavender bloom with purple markings unfolded. The flower caused an absolute sensation in Britain—a single bloom costing the equivalent of a hundred thousand dollars. Ironically, today that same orchid, named for its grower, *Cattleyea labiata autumnalis*, is one of the most popular and inexpensive corsage flowers in the world. Expeditions were quickly commissioned to seek out more of these precious flowers. It was a dangerous quest, since the tropics at the time were full of pitfalls—poisonous insects, deadly animals, and a host of diseases fatal to Westerners—not to mention the fact that many regions were inhabited by natives who didn't take kindly to outsiders.

For decades, orchids remained rare and precious due to their rather demanding culture requirements. The first explorers killed orchids by the boatloads. Very few of them survived the long voyages to Europe and America, and once here, they were often confined to stuffy, dark rooms which approximated the Victorian's mistaken concept of their original jungle climate. Thanks to modern propagation methods, such as tissue culture, have substantially lowered the price of production, plus a better understanding of orchid culture, today anyone—with or without a greenhouse—can enjoy the exotic pleasures of orchids.

and could accommodate a wide variety of plants, sometimes coming complete with aquariums.

For advice on making your own Wardian case, see page 117 in the appendix.

Arranging Flowers

The Victorian pastime of decorating rooms with flower arrangements goes back to the medieval era, when fragrant flowers and herbs, thought to clear the air of disease and pestilence, were strewn on floors and arranged in pots on windows to provide much needed relief indoors. By the Victorian era, of course, the practice had become purely decorative, and cut flowers were used as just another way to enliven the interior decor. At Point Ellice, Caroline gathered flowers from the gardens and the surrounding woods to display in vases throughout the house, to wear on her hat, or to give as gifts to friends and neighbors. Kathleen, especially, helped her mother with this pleasant task and would spend hours combing the nearby fields and woodlands gathering decorative wildflowers and mosses.

Caroline's taste in flower arrangements is not known, but if she followed general fashion, colors probably ran to the bold. Brightly hued plants from all over the world such as gladiola from South Africa, dahlias and nasturtiums from Mexico, and tree peonies from China had only recently been introduced, their novelty inspiring passionate enthusiasm for arranging them indoors. Strong color contrasts were favored, blue and orange or yellow and violet, with plenty of green foliage as a foil. Some designers, especially later in the century, argued for more sedate arrangements. William Robinson, in his 1883 work, *The English Flower Garden*, wrote that in arranging flowers one should "seek unity, harmony, and simplicity of effect rather than complexities, many of which involve much wearisome labour."

Elaborate table decorations like this example were standard fare for upper-class Victorian dinner parties.

Dressing for Success

Flowers, of course, were also very much part of the Victorian dress code. Single or sometimes even bunches of carnations were worn in the buttonhole of a proper gentleman. Ladies too would adorn themselves with flowers. On special occasions, elaborate headdresses, such as wreaths of mayflowers, roses, or lily blossoms, would be intricately woven into the wearer's hair, the goal being to keep the arrangement looking regal, but not make it too clumsy or heavy for the wearer. Ingenuity was also required to keep these personal adornments looking fresh through a long day of work or an extended formal event. Always resourceful, the Victorians developed a most useful device, a stem-sized glass tube filled with water that could be sealed with wax around the stem. Worn under the lapel in a tailored pocket or hidden in a lady's hair, the vial would keep a bloom fresh for hours.

Another trick of Victorian hairdressing involved backing floral headdresses with a strip of wool dabbed with isinglass, a glue prepared from fish air bladders. As the evening's festivities wore on, a lady's hairpiece remained looking vibrant, since the blossoms, despite the lack of water, could not droop.

The grandest of all personal adornments was the lady's bouquet. Evolving from the simple practice of gathering up and tying together a bunch of sweet-smelling flowers, called a nosegay, those arrangements soon were transformed into more complex "one-faced" constructions in which all flowers pointed in the same direction. These were easier for ladies to carry, especially in carriages, since they could lie on one's lap without being crushed. The center of a bouquet commonly contained a single large flower such as a white dahlia or peony, sur-

Kathleen, taken while visiting friends in England in the 1880s. Note the profuse use of flowers on her dress and fan.

rounded by smaller sprays of lilies, azaleas, or geraniums. The size of the arrangement was specifically tailored to fit the event. The largest was known as a presentation bouquet that was carried by a young lady being presented at Court. Wedding bouquets and shower bouquets were next in size. Interestingly, unlike brides of today, a proper Victorian woman would never think of throwing her bouquet into a crowd to be caught by eager-to-marry single women. This was considered far too risqué. The ball bouquet, the smallest and most common, was often carried by ladies to dress events such as dances and special functions. A number of them probably also were carried when the prime minister came to Point Ellice to tea—a fascinating tale to be told in the next chapter. *For tips on how to create a Victorian bouquet, see page 118 in the appendix*

What could be more delightful on a cold, wet winter's day than a chance brush against a dainty flowering houseplant that immediately fills the air with the sensuous scent of roses? It's not as impossible as you might think. All you need is a sunny windowsill and that Victorian favorite, the scented geranium. Not only are these plants easy to grow, but the beautiful, fragrant foliage and colorful flowers of scented geraniums make them true aristocrats of the container window garden.

Scented geraniums are actually not geraniums at all, but rather pelargoniums, members of the larger family of plants to which true geraniums also belong. They are native to Africa's Cape of Good Hope and were brought to Europe in the early 1600s, where they quickly became popular both as flowering plants and for their leaves, which were used (and still are) in astringents, potpourris, teas, and sachets. Scented geraniums were imported to this country in the Colonial era, and counted among their advocates none other than that great plantsman and American president Thomas Jefferson, who was responsible for the introduction of several new varieties.

Their greatest popularity came in the mid-1800s, when the French discovered a method of using the oil from scented geraniums in perfume, thereby creating a huge market for commercial production and propagation of new varieties. The number of new varieties exploded, and no Victorian garden worth its salt would have been without multiple scented geraniums, whether in the parlor as a houseplant, or outside, as fancy bedding plants in the border. Then, in the early part of the twentieth century, like many things Victorian, the plants fell from favor, and it was only through the dedicated work of a few determined growers that many of the older varieties survived.

Today, with the popularity of scented geraniums reviving, there are still well over a hundred varieties in common cultivation, sporting fragrances almost incredible to believe until you actually come in contact with them: lemon, pine, grape, nutmeg, coconut,

SCENTED GERANIUMS

chocolate, apple, peppermint, and even Old Spice, to name just a few. And their fragrance is not all they have to recommend them. Scented geraniums are handsome plants, most with beautiful, feathery, cut leaves (some with cream or white variegations) and delicate flowers (much smaller and more elegant than the common geraniums), ranging in color from white through deep lavender.

Few plants could be easier to grow. Scented geraniums, like their geranium cousins, are very tolerant of many adverse conditions and can survive up to several weeks without water. Scented geraniums should occupy a sunny window. They prefer daytime temperatures of about 65 to 70°F, with a drop of 10° or so at night. They are tender perennials, so if you choose to use them outside—which was very much the Victorian practice and highly recommended since they make great companion plants in annual borders, window boxes, and container gardens—be sure to bring them inside well before the first frost. Their one demand as houseplants is that they cannot stand wet feet, so water only when dry. Fertilize lightly every other month or so from March through November, but use a light touch. Too much nitrogen in the soil can actually diminish their fragrance. Scented geraniums are not susceptible to many pests if well grown, though sometimes in the winter, aphids or white flies can be an issue. If an insect problem occurs, take the plant, pot and all, and submerge in a tub with soapy water so that all the leaves are underwater for several hours. Remove and drain thoroughly before returning to the window sill. You can also spray as a last resort, but refrain from using insecticides if you are planning to harvest the leaves for tea or potpourri.

Scented geraniums can be easily started from cuttings. Simply snip off a 3- to 4-inch stem, remove any leaves or branches on the lower 2 inches, dip into a rooting hormone, and place the cutting in a damp, soilless mixture. Keep in semishade until the roots develop, and three to four weeks later you should have a new little plant ready for transplanting.

So the next time a gloomy day has you down, venture forth for a few scented geraniums and give yourself a breath of spring!

For a list of Victorian-era scented geranium varieties, see page 119 in the appendix.

CHAPTER V

GRACIOUS LIVING IN THE GARDEN

Preparing for the Fete • The Sporting Life • Dinner and the Garden • PLANTS WITH A PAST: Lilacs

In the summer of 1886, Point Ellice House was abuzz with excitement. Over the years, Caroline had hosted many functions at her home, a number of which were socially important enough to rate a mention in the local newspaper, *The Daily Colonist*. But this was different: The most important man in the land, the prime minister of Canada, was coming for high tea on Tuesday. Sir John McDonald and his wife, Lady McDonald, and their entourage had arrived from the nation's capital the week before and had been touring Vancouver Island, much of the time probably accompanied by the provincial governor, and Caroline's brother, John Trutch. That they would make time for tea in the gardens of Point Ellice was testament to the growing influence of the O'Reilly family in local business and political circles.

> In asking people to dine, you should put to yourself the question, "Why do I ask them?" and unless the answer is satisfactory, they are not likely to contribute much to the agreeability and sociality of the conviviality.
>
> —A. V. KIRWAN,
> *Host and Guest*

For middle-class Victorians, entertaining provided an important means of expanding one's circle and climbing up the social ladder. For Peter, who was often away on business, entertaining was easy. All he had to do was show up. For Caroline, though, it was a very different story. In addition to managing the Point Ellice household, which included tending to all the domestic chores as well as the animals and garden, in Peter's absence Caroline was in charge of the family's social schedule. This life revolved around a tight circle of expatriate English families, who tended to mingle principally with one another. While Point Ellice House was by no means the largest or most elegant house in Victoria, the added appeal of its gardens provided a lavish backdrop for endless games of croquet, lawn tennis tournaments, tea parties, and other outdoor gatherings. It seemed that Caroline was hosting an afternoon tea, of varying size, almost every day. There were plenty of informal gatherings as well. Close friends and relatives were welcome to stop by unannounced, leading to spontaneous gatherings such as picnics that were part of the delightful life at Point Ellice.

Regardless of the event, rules of etiquette reigned supreme, and dinner parties, teas, and even simple croquet games were conducted with the proper attention to detail. Food, dress, china, and even the furnishings were all dictated by Vic-

torian social norms. Caroline was trained in the proper execution of each event and took pains to make them as flawless as possible, for nothing reflected as poorly on a family as an ill-planned party. The reception for the McDonalds would have to be perfect.

Today, we tend to have picnics outside and parties inside. Part of this preference likely has to do with our ability to control the indoor environment, but there's another factor at work. These days we tend to think of our house and garden as two separate, unrelated parts of the property. Such a dis-

The O'Reillys enjoyed entertaining in their garden, offering high tea to their guests or playing a game of lawn tennis or croquet. Point Ellice teas were so memorable, in fact, that Robert Scott, the famous Antarctic explorer once entertained there, sent Kathleen and Mrs. O'Reilly a tea set, which still remains in the collection.

tinction, however, was completely foreign to the Victorians. In fact, in the nineteenth century the landscape was truly considered an extension of indoor living space and as such, on nice days, it wouldn't be unusual for a hostess like Caroline to use her garden for that quintessentially British custom of "taking tea," setting up refreshments both inside and out so that guests might flow between house and garden as they wished. At Point Ellice, outdoor teas were generally held on the croquet lawn to afford guests the best view of the garden and the Selkirk Water beyond.

Preparing for the Fete

Each season was marked by frantic displays intended to impress the right people, so no setting seemed more conspicuous than the lawn or garden. Receptions, recitals, and tea parties were precisely planned to convey the proper image.

—M. CHRISTINE KLIM DOELL,
Gardens of the Gilded Age

This brass tea kettle and stand were a presentation piece given to Arthur O'Reilly by the men who served under his command at Newport. When in use, the small spirit lamp kept the water hot, allowing the hostess to add it to the teapot as needed.

We can only imagine the planning that went into a tea held for the prime minister because the O'Reillys, normally so loquacious in their writings, were probably just too busy to keep up their usual prolific journal entries. But we do know that the event would have followed a very precise form. Weeks before the party, Caroline, as hostess, would have sent handwritten invitations to her guests announcing the tea. Although much simpler than a formal dinner, an elaborate meal would have to be planned. The food served at an afternoon tea, whether held indoors or in the garden, was dictated by the hour. The earlier the event, the lighter the fare, but it almost always included tea cakes, waffles and muffins, preserved fruits, and biscuits. Caroline's favorite was the lemon-curd tart. Point Ellice visitors would also snack on watercress or cucumber sandwiches and a variety of cakes. A simple, family-only tea might feature merely some homemade jam made with fruit picked from the garden, spread on home-baked bread. If the tea began as late as four or five in the afternoon, Caroline might serve slices of baked ham, grilled chicken, or head cheese on sandwiches. All of the food would have been laid on a large table, draped with the good afternoon-tea tablecloth. The sweets would have been set out on special cake dishes and placed on Caroline's elegant, multitiered cake stand. It was all designed to impress, as well as nourish.

On the day of the event, Caroline almost certainly would have had her servants carefully clean her best afternoon tea china—creamy white with delicate images of poppies, irises, and peonies.

Caroline, as was the Victorian norm, owned many sets of china, including a number of tea services. The best were saved for the most important guests or for the most formal occasions. There was also a set for each meal. The breakfast dishes were never used for dinner, which was usually eaten at midday, and the tea services were reserved only for that special afternoon ritual. On the tea table, a small plate, a knife, a napkin, and a cup and saucer for each guest would have been carefully arranged.

As the hour drew near, the guests began to arrive. There were a few score, plus the prime minister, an unusually large gathering for an afternoon tea. Guests at such functions would normally stay for less than an hour, although the entire event might have lasted for two or three. Gossip, along with events of the day, would be exchanged informally. Unfortunately, we have little information on how the O'Reillys fared at the actual tea attended by the prime minister. However, with Caroline's practiced social graces and with the Point Ellice gardens as an impressive backdrop, it is highly likely that the affair was a huge success.

For advice on hosting a Victorian garden tea party, see pages 122–23 in the appendix.

The Sporting Life

As part of afternoon tea at Point Ellice, guests might find themselves cajoled into a game of croquet or lawn tennis. Very soon after buying the house, Peter installed a croquet ground, and the family began avidly to indulge in this fashionable Victorian sport.

It was not just the O'Reillys who were caught up in the croquet craze. The game, introduced in England in 1856, spread quickly to America as well. It was the perfect pastime for garden parties, be-

A Victorian-era lawn tennis set.

The children and I went to see Mrs Drake and after sitting a little, she asked us to stay and take tea. I did not want to stay but I thought it would seem friendly, so I agreed... The piano is very bad and they are both very uninteresting people. We left at 10 o'clock. They did not offer us any other refreshments, but Mr Drake walked home with us to the door and told us a story of this house having been once entered by a burglar, which was not very well timed...

The O'Reilly and Trutch families playing the Victorian national pastime, croquet, at the Trutch family home in Fairfield. Caroline appears to be instructing five-year-old Frank while Kathleen stands beside her father, who is seated on the lawn.

family for a rigorous game of croquet and an afternoon tea party. The men donned their croquet whites, an ensemble of white cotton pants, a white shirt, a cap, and even special croquet shoes. The women put on their finest tea dresses for the day of celebration. Usually a white or other pale hue, the garments would be topped off with a beautiful garden hat to keep their feminine complexions the Victorian standard of creamy white.

By the 1880s, lawn tennis had also burst onto the scene as another of the social sporting activities so enjoyed by the Victorians. Soon after it was introduced to North America in 1874, the Point Ellice croquet ground could be found draped with the requisite tennis net. Unlike the game played today, tennis began as a calm sport, with delicate volleys that

cause both sexes could play, creating a ready excuse for meeting the opposite sex. In fact, one early rule book states that "women are fond of cheating at the game, but they do so only because men like it." Our first truly national sport, croquet became so popular in North America that hardly a humble garden existed that didn't dedicate at least a small patch of lawn to it, and manufacturers even sold sets with candle sockets on the wickets for playing after dark.

At least one O'Reilly family member, Jack, became good enough to win a number of croquet tournaments. Once a year, the O'Reillys hosted a tournament of their own. Every May Day (May 24, the celebration of Queen Victoria's birthday) as parades, regattas, and celebrations took place all over the city, the O'Reillys invited their friends and

Never one to miss a social event, Kathleen O'Reilly, in white, standing on the dock under the parasol, watches the 1894 Selkirk Regatta.

Above: Kathleen, pictured with Frank, Jack, and guests. Peter and Caroline are sitting on the bench. The date is about 1891 or 1892, during the "season," when Kathleen spent every evening at a ball, her dance card full of the names of Royal Navy officers.

Below: A game of lawn tennis over, a commemorative photograph was taken at Point Ellice, about 1882.

protected the sanctity of the female body. M. Christine Klim Doell writes in *Gardens of the Gilded Age*, that "it was meant to provide summer afternoon sport that was not too active for ladies in toe-length dresses." Within a few decades, however, practitioners of the sport developed a com-

petitive edge, and the game moved from backyard landscapes to the professionally manicured lawns that still make up many of the tennis courts today.

For advice on playing croquet the Victorian way, see pages 124–25 in the appendix.

Dinner and the Garden

Of late years it has been the custom to ornament the dinner-table either with living plants or cut-flowers, or the two tastefully combined, and we can but endeavour to encourage and promote this elegant innovation.

—F. W. BURBIDGE

Teas weren't the only meal with a garden theme. Dinners, especially formal dinner parties, borrowed from the garden as well. Upper-class families used the affairs to consolidate their position in society, and an invitation to dine was an opportunity to initiate or strengthen a social bond between host and guest. For these reasons, and because the O'Reillys loved to entertain, there were frequent formal gatherings at Point Ellice. As with her garden tea parties, Caroline took great pains to make sure every aspect of a meal was perfectly prepared and presented. Perhaps in recognition of her beautiful gardens, or because it had become the Victorian norm, Caroline often elected to decorate the dining room with flowers. In the dining room window, Caroline placed her geraniums, maidenhair fern, hyacinths, and narcissus on simple cedar stands. On the dinner table itself, Caroline often used glass vases with small rose buds, lily of the valley, or snowdrops as a centerpiece. She also had a set of porcelain menu card holders—elaborate menus were a must at such functions—with tiny bud vases positioned on each side.

Dinner-table decorations at the O'Reillys were elegant, but still modest compared to some upper-class Victorian households. Imagine walking into a Victorian dining room and discovering a table full of food nestled amongst an elaborate display of flowers and foliage. Such arrangements might include a graceful arch of fuchsia or white Chilean bellflowers, neatly mounted on wire and offset by ferns or ornamental grasses. Burbidge, whose *Domestic Floriculture* was one of the chief style guides of the day, calls for "bold flowers of graceful form and decided colors." Sprays of jasmine, he notes, as well as some orchids, are "very chaste and beautiful. . . . Preference should always be given to large flowers of decided shades of red or to those of pearly whiteness. These show well and never fail to please when tastefully set off with fresh green ferns."

Such a setting might also include a tall, ornate epergne as a centerpiece, spilling over with flowers from the dishes sitting on its tiered arms and surrounded by candles. It would be set above eye level so as not to impede dinner conversation. Interestingly, such arrangements were often scentless so as to not compete with the aroma of dinner. Another common, rather simple arrangement included a row of three flower vases, the central one a few inches taller than the others, containing lilies or roses. A grander presentation might include a small forest of palms as the centerpiece with smaller plants or cut flowers in front of each place. Adventurous hosts could even create an arch over the dinner table made from wire and stretched from end to end; the span would then be painstakingly covered with long twines of ivy or other attractive foliage.

Concealing the mechanics of these arrangements with ferns or other greenery was an important element of the design. The table was to appear as "naturally" verdant as possible. Some Victorians especially eager to impress guests went so far as to have pots built into their tables so that flowers would appear to spring miraculously from the surface. For those who decided to forgo cutting holes in expensive tables and eschewed heavy use of concealing foliage, highly decorative containers called cachepots—the only ones considered suitable to stand alone—were also available, though certain color rules prevailed. "White and pale blue enameled kinds may be tolerated, but gaudy affairs of crimson, purple, scarlet, or gold should be avoided," stated Burbidge. Despite the work and time involved, the O'Reillys never flagged in their desire to entertain properly. Nor were they just following custom. For the O'Reillys, a good dinner party, a proper afternoon tea, or a lively game of croquet were some of the most enjoyable aspects of life in the Victorian age.

CAROLINE TO PETER—3 MAY 1873

The garden is still looking very pretty. The lilacs are coming into bloom. I am afraid they will have passed off before you can return.

Of all the different shrubs visitors today enjoy in the Point Ellice gardens, lilacs are perhaps the most numerous; they occur in all parts of the grounds in many different varieties and must have been a spectacular sight during the O'Reillys' frequent springtime croquet parties and outdoor teas. Interestingly, the profusion of lilacs we now take for granted is actually a Victorian invention, and can be traced directly back to the singular obsession of one of the period's most remarkable gardening teams.

Although the lilac had been around for centuries, the first specimen of *Syringa vulgaris* (the common lilac) was brought to Vienna from the Court of Suleiman the Magnificent in Constantinople in 1562, and rapidly spread throughout Europe and North America. The number of new lilac cultivars remained quite small for several centuries. Then fate intervened: In 1870, during the Franco-Prussian War, the Germans overran the northern portion of France, including the town of Nancy, home to the famous nursery of Victor Lemoine et Fils. According to the story, Monsieur Lemoine, with his trade pretty much idled for the duration, had decided to pass his time trying to breed a good double lilac. M. Lemoine, however, had very poor eyesight, a true disability for anyone interested in pollinating the tiny individual flowers of the lilac, and so it fell to poor

Madame Lemoine to stand for hours on a ladder, petticoats fluttering in the wind, gently pollinating selected shrubs. Fortunately for us she persevered, and between 1876 and 1927, the firm introduced over 153 named cultivars, many of which remain garden favorites to this day. This and subsequent breeding programs, including several

LILACS

concentrated efforts to spread the shrub's range both north and south, combined with the introduction of new species from China around the turn of the century, mean that today's selection of lilacs now numbers well over two thousand.

Lilacs are extremely easy to grow in Zones 3 to 7, as long as they are given full sun (at least seven hours of direct sunlight a day) and a slightly alkaline soil. The old Victorian trick of adding several handfuls of wood ash once a year to your lilacs works quite well to maintain the pH at proper levels. With lilacs, do be careful about pruning. Lilacs bloom on last year's wood, and any cutting done much after bloom time will limit next year's flowering. If like many people you have inherited an old scraggly shrub in need of rejuvenation, the best way to pro-

ceed is to cut back a third of the old woody growth each year. This method forces the shrub to send out new sucker growth to reinvigorate the clump.

For a truly Victorian feel in your garden, try some of these cultivars, many of which were Lemoine introductions, and most of which are still easy to track down:

'Alphonse Lavellee' (1885) double lilac
'Belle de Nancy' (1891) double pink
'Cavour' (1910) single violet
'Charles Joly' (1896) double magenta
'Charles X' (1830) single magenta
'Christophe Colomb' (1905) single lilac
'Congo' (1896) single magenta
'De Miribel' (1903) single violet
'De Saussure' (1903) double purple
'Decaisne' (1910) single blue
'Ellen Willmott' (1903) double white
'Jacques Callot' (1876) single lilac
'Jeanne d'Arc' (1902) double white
'Leon Gambetta' (1907) double lilac
'Lucie Balter' (1888) single pink
'Ludwig Spaeth' (1883) single purple
'Macrostachya' (1844) single pink
'Marc Micheli' (1898) double pink
'Marie Legraye' (1879) single white
'Mme Antoine Buckner' (1909) double pink
'Mme Lemoine' (1890) double white
'Mme Casimir Perier' (1894) double white
'Mme F. Morel' (1892) single magenta
'Mme Florent Stepman' (1908) single white
'Monge' (1913) single purple
'Mont Blanc' (1910) single white
'Olivier de Serres' (1909) double blue
'Paul Harriot' (1902) double purple
'President Carnot' (1890) double lilac
'President Grevy' (1886) double blue
'Reamur' (1904) single magenta
'Victor Lemoine' (1906) double lilac
'Waldeck-Rosseau' (1904) double pink

CHAPTER VI
THE GARDEN PRODUCTIVE

Sea Changes in the Garden

It's hard for us to believe, surrounded by millions of decorative landscapes whose sole existence is merely to please, that these purely ornamental gardens are a remarkably recent introduction. It wasn't until after World War II, in fact, with the rise of cheap transit that could move edibles quickly and inexpensively over vast distances, that the home landscape surrendered its role as one of the principal means of producing food for the household. Until that time, it was commonplace, indeed often essential, that the home grounds should produce a large amount of the fresh produce the family consumed. Fruits and vegetables, especially those transported over vast distances, were expensive and hard to come by; additionally, many types of foodstuffs were only available in a limited season, unless someone in the household, usually the wife, took the time and trouble to put up and preserve what was grown at home.

This meant that in the Victorian era, unless you lived in a town house in the center of one of the few large cities like London or New York, you almost certainly had a kitchen garden. If you were extremely wealthy, you often had one on your country estate, which sent you fresh produce several times a week by train. Filled with fruits, vegetables, and often flowers for the table as well, these productive kitchen gardens were the heart and soul of the Victorian landscape. Daily life literally revolved around the sequence of products that flowed from the kitchen garden. What appeared on your table was by and large determined by what you grew. From the first radishes and spring greens, to the last frost-coated apple or leek, your garden was your larder. Given this direct link to the stomach, it's no surprise then that the Victori-

Above: The vegetable garden in early summer. The south garden, where the current vegetable plot lies, by and large still awaits final restoration. The vegetable plantings visitors see today are meant only as a suggestion of the area's original use.

Below: Sunflowers and cosmos reach for the sun in the cutting and vegetable garden.

ans, the O'Reillys included, were avid kitchen gardeners.

Modern Considerations

Before we take a detailed look at the Point Ellice House garden, some of you might be wondering what relevance, other than fascinatingly quaint historical discovery, the Victorian kitchen garden could hold for us today—especially given the fact that we do have frozen vegetables, readily available canned goods, and fresh produce available throughout the year. The answer is simple—cost and quality. Unless you live right next door to a farm that sends you produce daily for pennies on the dollar, there is no way you can buy anything near the quality of what you can grow at home yourself, all for the cost of some seeds or a few plants and a few hours of your labor. One tomato bush can yield bushels of mouthwatering fruit. An apple tree, once planted, will bear fruit of almost unimaginable flavor for fifty years or more. A row of raspberries will produce pint after pint of mouthwatering, expensive dainties all summer long. And of course for those of you concerned about pesticides in your food, in your own kitchen garden, you control what you use. Organic or inorganic, it's up to you.

Three varieties of Victorian cherries: 1. 'Early Rivers'; 2. 'Emperor Francis'; 3. 'White Bigarreau.'

From asparagus for your spring table to zinnias for a late summer bouquet, the kitchen garden can produce delights for both eyes and palette. Of course, there is labor involved, and if you're not inclined toward working in your garden, perhaps the supermarket is indeed a better option for you. But for those with a bit of time and inclination, a kitchen garden can produce a harvest of wonders.

Siting the Garden

The kitchen garden at Point Ellice was one of the most prominent elements of the entire landscape, and most likely, one of the first to be installed. In constructing his garden, Peter seemed to have followed almost to the letter the guidebooks of the day. Manuals such as *The Gardener's Assistant*, written by Robert Thompson in 1859 and regularly revised and expanded over the next sixty years, dedicates the entire second volume of some six hundred pages to the subject, giving a great deal of attention to the siting and layout of such gardens.

According to Thompson, a person interested in establishing a kitchen garden should seek ground that is either level or sloping gently to the south,

If you've never eaten an heirloom apple, then you have only experienced a fraction of the taste sensation apples have to offer. Pictured here: 'Gasocyne's Scarlet'; 'Charels Ross'; 'Allington Pippin'.

southeast, or southwest. Steep slopes were to be avoided, as well as low-lying areas since:

> . . . subsoil in such places being usually damp and sour, and it cannot be easily drained. Hoarfrost also prevails on such spots, and it often proves ruinous to crops. . . . An excellent form of garden is one with a regular declivity from north to south, in which direction a walk divided the area into two equal portions, each of which slopes uniformly from the side inwards to the central walk. The garden is thus generally inclined to the south, whilst the one half has an

PETER TO CAROLINE (FROM NEW WESTMINSTER)—16 JUNE 1874

"Kiss the dear Puss [Kathleen] for me and thank her for the strawberries she gathered... Don't forget to send for some bran for the Cow... Do all you can to have the water saved for the flowers and trees—I forgot to put the covers around the roots of the creepers under the box window—have them well watered and covered in the daytime...and do attend to the vegetables and eat them."

eastern inclination, the other a western. In this way the sun's rays have greater effect, and water runs off freely, but not too rapidly.

How the garden related to the rest of the landscape was also an important consideration.

If the mansion [Victorian gardening books almost always presumed wealth] is already built [as was the case at Point Ellice], and the ornamental grounds laid out, the fruit and vegetable garden should be placed in the best situation that the circumstances permit . . . and masked from view from the principal windows and front of the mansion either by natural undulations of the ground or by plantations of trees and shrubs. It should be screened from view from the pleasure grounds by the same means, as well as from the main carriage drives. The distance at which it may be placed must depend upon the size of the mansion

and the extent of the surrounding pleasure grounds . . . but a shorter distance is desirable, both for the convenience of the proprietor and for the easy transfer of the garden produce to the mansion.

As to shape, rectangles were the favored design for kitchen gardens, preferably in the ratio of three to five. This is interesting because it's one of the few times that the Victorians allowed their love of curves to take second stage to pure practicality. Squared beds and paths were judged easiest to work and maintain.

In planning walks for the fruit and kitchen garden, utility ought to be the leading principle; whilst regularity should be kept in view as much as possible. With regard to their number and direction, the necessity of a path all round, so as to leave a border of greater or lesser width between it and the walls (or hedges) is universally admitted; and two paths intersecting each other in the center of the garden are found convenient. This arrangement is very generally adopted. Besides these principal walks, two or more subordinate ones . . . may be necessary; but the number and disposition depends upon the extent and form of the ground.

The kitchen garden in early spring. Hundreds of bulbs bloom while a young fruit tree is about to burst into leaf. No one has yet figured out the purpose of the twigs lain across the path. Any ideas, gentle reader? It was this picture, with the hint of the fence post revealed in the far corner, that allowed the authors a rethinking and newly proposed reconstruction of the south garden.

At Point Ellice, Peter followed such advice almost to the letter. For the location, he chose the sunniest site possible, a site that sloped gently to the southwest and drained easily and well.

Drainage was and is a critical issue in kitchen gardens, especially in extremely rainy climates like Victoria's. Too much water held in the soil will simply rot the roots of the plants. (To learn more about preparing the soil for the kitchen garden, follow the instructions found in chapter III.) In proper fashion, Peter's garden was surrounded by hedges on the north side—Lawson cypress (*Chamaecyparis lawsoniana*) along the drive, and by cherry laurel (*Prunus laurocerasus*) and hawthorn (*Crataegus spp.*) along the border near the house. Not only did this serve to separate the utilitarian areas from the ornamental, but such "plantations" had the added benefit of protecting the gardens from harsh winds and sudden temperature changes, as the advice of the day advocated.

Seen in the spring of 1902, the north-south pathway through the kitchen garden overflows with flowers, fruits, and vegetables.

Layout and Design

In regard to the walks, Peter modified the general guidelines to accommodate the specifics of his site. A large north-south walk intersects a path that presumably extended originally around the perimeter. When we say "presumably," it's with good reason. The exact configuration of the path layout in the Point Ellice House kitchen garden has been the topic of considerable debate, although it seems pretty clear that the modern state of the garden is only vaguely correct. The area has yet to be fully restored. From the existing photographic evidence, it's known with certainty that the north-south walk existed, as well as two principal east-west paths that ran along the southerly and northerly sides of the garden. What happened

PETER TO CAROLINE—2 JULY 1871

Before leaving I forgot to ask you for the recipe for making pea soup, you recollect I bought some split peas. Mashell has tried to cook them twice but it proved a failure. I think he must have boiled them for 24 hours, but he could not succeed in making them soft and the soup was like water. Anything of this sort makes a change, one gets so very tired of beans and bacon every day. The water is too high and muddy to catch fish as yet, and there is no game to be had at this season.

along the far east and west sides is not so obvious. Archaeological evidence is missing or inconclusive, and the photographic record only shows hints of these walks (see Chapter VIII). The subject is further clouded by the later 1890s addition of the greenhouse in the kitchen-garden area, along with cold frames (both regrettably now missing but hopefully soon to be restored) that would have necessitated the alteration of the earlier path layout. The smaller, subsidiary paths that would have certainly subdivided the larger areas and given access to the interior of the beds were most likely made of packed earth or mulch moved and altered with each new season.

Fruits and Vegetables Grown at Point Ellice

The O'Reillys were avid vegetable gardeners, and their correspondence is full of references not only to the kitchen garden, but also to the field across the street where they grew other larger-scale crops such as potatoes, squash, and corn, as well as fodder crops for their animals. Peter issued a constant stream of directives in the form of long letters to Caroline urging her to tend to soil improvement (a constant concern where high productivity was required; see Chapter III on manures), crop planting, weeding, watering, harvesting, and storage. She dutifully complied and reported her successes and failures in her replies. From this correspondence and other archival records, we are able to pinpoint with remarkable accuracy what crops were grown at Point Ellice.

What follows is a list of vegetables known to have been grown at Point Ellice, with appropriate growing instructions for each taken from Peter Henderson's 1893 work *Gardening for Pleasure*, still remarkably pertinent and practical more than 125 years after it was first published. Any modern comments or clarifications appear in brackets. It should be noted that wherever Henderson refers to latitude in his directions, he means the area around New York, which in today's gardening parlance would be Zone 6B/7A. Readers north or south of this zone will need to adjust the timing of his advice accordingly. Additionally, the quantity of seed listed by Henderson is meant to supply the complete yearly needs of a family of five. Modern gardeners may wish to start on a much smaller scale.

For modern versions of recipes from Caroline's kitchen, see page 130 in the appendix.

ASPARAGUS

Asparagus should be planted the first spring that the owner comes into possession of the land. In the latitude of New York, any time from April 1 to May 15th; and if the house is yet to be built, let the asparagus bed be planted at once, as it takes the roots two to three years to acquire sufficient strength to give a crop. For an ordinary family, a bed of six rows of fifty or sixty feet in length, and three feet apart will be sufficient [One row would probably be more than enough for a modern family.] The preparation of the asparagus bed should be made with more care than for most vegetables, from the fact that it is a permanent crop, which ought to yield as well at the end of 25 years as of 5 years, if the soil has been well prepared the plants in the rows being set nine inches apart. In planting, it is customary to use two-year-old plants.

BEANS (BROAD)

An indispensable vegetable, of easy cultivation, growing freely in almost any soil, though in well-enriched land it will be more prolific in quantity and more tender in quality. It is a plant of tropical origin, and, like all such, should not be sown until the weather is settled and warm, and all danger from frost is past. In this latitude, the time of sowing should not be sooner than the fifth of May. Sow at intervals of two or three weeks all through the season, if wanted for use. Seed may be sown in drills eighteen to twenty-four inches apart, and three inches deep, dropping the seeds at distances of two or three inches in the drills, and covering to the general level. For such as use them all through the season, three or four quarts of seed would be required, although a quart at one sowing would give an ample quantity for any average family.

BEANS (RUNNER)

Pole Beans are usually cultivated in hills three or four feet apart. The poles (which are best made of young cedar trees [long bamboo stakes work equally well]) should be nine or ten feet high, and firmly fixed at least eighteen inches deep in the ground, and the hills formed around them by digging up the soil and mixing it with a shovelful of well-rotted manure, or an ounce or so of guano or bone-dust, if stable manure is not attainable [compost would work equally well]; but in either case let the mixing be thorough. The hills should be but two or three inches above the general level, and at least eighteen inches in diameter. The term "hill" is an unfortunate one, as it often leads inexperienced persons to suppose that a tall heap must be made, and it is a common mistake to form miniature hills often a foot or more in height, upon which to sow seeds or set plants. The effect of this is to confine the roots to this small, high and dry space. When the word "hill" is used in this work, it is to indicate the place plants are to occupy, and unless some height is mentioned, it is not above the general level. After the hill has been properly formed around the pole, from five to six beans should be planted around it at a depth of two inches; but the planting should never be done in this latitude before the 20th of May . . . All kinds of running and pole beans have been usually grown on poles eight or ten feet long; but the new pea vine trellis, introduced in 1887, is infinitely better and far more convenient.

BEETS

Sow in shallow drills twelve to eighteen inches apart in April or May, dropping the seeds so that they will fall an inch or so apart. When the plants have grown to the height of about two inches, thin out, so that they will stand four inches apart. When the roots are three inches in diameter they are fit for use. Of course they are used when much larger, but the younger they are, the more delicate and tender. Four ounces will be sufficient for ordinary family

THE LOST GARDEN ART OF BLANCHING

Mention the term blanching today, and you are more than likely to think of the quick steaming process good chefs commonly use to fix color and crispness in green vegetables like beans or broccoli. A hundred years or so ago, the phrase was equally ubiquitous, but with an entirely different meaning. To the Victorians, blanching referred to the common practice of whitening (from the French *blancher*, to whiten) vegetables by piling up mounds of earth around them, or enclosing them in specially made containers to exclude the light, a number of which still survive at Point Ellice. The result was plants with pale, tender stalks and leaves that were thought to have far superior texture and flavor than those grown under normal light.

A surprising number of vegetables that today we wouldn't think twice about using in their natural state, such as celery and asparagus, were considered unfit for consumption unless blanched. Also generally blanched were rhubarb, sea kale (*Crambe maritima*) and cardoon (*Cynara cardunculus*), the last two being Victorian favorites that have almost largely disappeared from the modern table. Often the process of blanching was combined with forcing by placing a plant such as rhubarb under a specially made pot, and piling the pot high with fresh manure. The insulating effect of the mound, combined with the heat given off by the decomposing manure, artificially warmed the plant under the pot, allowing growth in all but the most severe weather.

Both of these customs gradually fell into disuse due to changes in taste and technology. The rise of modern transport made it cheaper to bring in produce from warmer climates than it was to force your own. Blanching, whose main purpose was to tenderize otherwise tough varieties, was largely supplanted by more naturally tender cultivars and improved cooking techniques that allowed for better texture and flavor retention. Today, the only blanched vegetable still found on our tables, especially in Europe, is asparagus. So far are we removed from this once-common practice that many people are convinced that the white stalks on their plates are an entirely different species, rather than simply the product of the age-old process of blanching.

use, unless successive crops are wanted, when double the quantity may be used.

BROCCOLI

We persist in growing under the distinct names of Broccoli and Cauliflower, plants which at best are nothing more than very nearly related varieties. [Henderson's comment here is interesting: a century of breeding has certainly made broccoli distinct from cauliflower these days, but evidently in the late 1800's, this wasn't the case.] The main difference between them is, that what we call broccoli is planted for fall use, while that which we call cauli-

flower is planted for spring or summer use; though in this respect they are frequently reversed without seeming to mind it. For fall use a packet of seed should be sown in the early part of May, which will give plants large enough to be set out in July. Further south the sowing of the seed should be delayed from four to six weeks later, and the plants to be set out correspondingly later . . . The plants are set at two and a half to three feet apart, and as a hundred plants are all that most families would use, it is usually cheaper to buy them, if in a section where they are sold, than to raise the plants from seed. Broccoli requires an abundance of manure.

CABBAGE

The cabbage is so easily raised that but little space need be devoted to it here. Like all of its tribe, it requires an abundance of manure for its full development. The early varieties should be either raised in cold frames or in hot beds as stated for cauliflower, and planted out at distances of from twenty to thirty inches apart each way, as early as the ground is fit to work in April . . . For the late varieties, the seed should be sown in May, and the plants set out in June or July at two to three feet apart.

CARROTS

Carrots are sown any time from April to June, in rows one foot apart covering the seed two inches deep. If the soil is light, they will be better flavored. When the plants are an inch or so high, thin out to three or four inches apart. . . . Eight ounces of seed will sow three hundred feet of row, which, for most families, would be an abundance, both for summer and winter use. Carrots are much prized as food for horses and cows, and if wanted for this purpose in quantity, they should be sown with a seed-drill, in rows one and a half

to two feet apart. About four pounds of seed per acre are required.

CAULIFLOWER

I will briefly state how early Cauliflowers can be most successfully grown here. First, the soil must be well broken and pulverized by spading or plowing to at least a foot in depth, mixing through it a layer of three or four inches of strong, well-rotted stable manure. The plants may be either those from seed sown last fall and wintered over in cold frames, or else started from seeds sown in January or February, in a hot-bed or greenhouse, and planted in small pots or boxes, so as to make plants strong enough to be set out as soon as the soil is fit to work, which in this latitude is usually the first week in April. We are often applied to for Cauliflower plants as late as the end of May, but the chances of their forming heads when planted late in May are slim indeed.

The surest way to secure the heading of Cauliflowers is to use what are called hand-glasses. . . . These are usually made about two feet square, which gives room enough for three or four plants of Cauliflower, until they are so far forwarded that the glass can be taken off. When the hand glass is used, the Cauliflowers may be planted out in any warm border early in March and covered by them. This covering protects them from frosts at night, and gives the necessary increase of temperature for growth during the cold weeks of March and April; so that by the first week in May, if the Cauliflower has been properly hardened off by ventilating (by tilting up the hand-glasses on one side), they may be taken off alto-gether. . . . If the weather is dry, the Cauliflowers will be much benefited by being thoroughly soaked with water twice or thrice a week; not a mere sprinkling, which is of no use, but a complete drenching, so that the water will reach to the lowest roots. If the ground is slightly sprinkled around the roots with guano before watering, all the better.

CELERY

The seeds are sown on a well pulverized, rich border, in the open ground, as early in the season as the ground can be worked. The bed is kept clear of weeds until July, when the plants are set out for the crop. But as the seedling plants are rather troublesome to raise, the small number wanted for private use can usually be purchased cheaper than they can be raised on a small scale (they cost from fifty cents to a dollar per hundred); and if they can be procured fresh from the seedsmen, market gardeners, or florists in the neighborhood, it is never worth while to sow the seed, as from three hundred to five hundred plants are ample for ordinary sized families. . . .

Celery is a "gross feeder," and requires two to three inches thick of well-rotted manure, which, as usual, must be well mixed and incorporated with the soil before the celery is set out. If stable manure is not convenient, bone dust, guano, or other concentrated fertilizer may be sown on the rows about as thick as sand or sawdust is strewn on the floor, and well chopped in and mixed with the soil. Whether stable manure or a concentrated fertilizer be used, it should be spread over and mixed to at least twelve inches in width and six inches in depth. When the ground is thus prepared we stretch a line to the distance required, and beat it slightly with a spade, so that it leaves a mark to show where to place the plants. These are set out at distances of six inches between the plants, and usually four feet between the rows. Great care must be taken in putting out the celery, to see that the plant is set just to the depth of the roots. If much deeper, the "heart" might be too much covered up, which would impede the growth. It is also important that the soil be well packed to the root in planting; and if the operation can be done in the evening, and the plants copiously watered, no further watering will usually be required.

If planted in July, nothing is to be done but keep the crop clear of weeds until September. By that time the handling process is to be begun, which consists in drawing the earth to each side of the Celery, and pressing it tightly to it, so as to give the leaves an upward growth preparatory to blanching for use. Supposing this handling process is done by the middle of September, by the first week in October it is ready for "banking up," which is done by digging the soil from between the rows and laying or banking it up on each side of the row of Celery. After being so banked up in October, it will be ready for use in three or four weeks.

CORN

The varieties known as "Sweet" are the kinds cultivated to be used in the green state [i.e., eaten fresh]. Corn may either be planted in "hills" (dropping three or four seeds in a hill) four feet apart each way, or in rows five feet apart, dropping the seeds at distances of eight or ten inches in the rows. In this latitude it is useless to plant Corn before the middle of May. For successive crops it should be planted every two or three weeks until July first. After that date it will not mature here. Corn requires a rich, light soil to be early.

CRESS

A spring and summer salad plant. Sow in early spring, and in succession every week or so if desired, in rows one foot apart. The curled variety is the best, as it can be used for garnishing as well as for salad.

CUCUMBER

In most places where the cucumber is grown outdoors, it is more or less troubled with the "Striped Bug," but if only a few dozen hills are cultivated it is not a very troublesome matter to pick them off, which is about the only sure way to get rid of them. The safest method of raising cucumbers, however, is to cover the seeds, when first sown, with the hand-glass . . . which by the time they are wanted for cucumbers, are no longer needed for cauliflowers. If such hand-glasses are not obtainable, a simple method is to use a light box ten or twelve inches square, and place it over the seeds after sowing, covering it with a pane of glass. This will not only forward the germination of the seeds, but will protect the plants against the bugs until they are strong enough not to be injured by them. . . . Light sandy soil is rather best for cucumbers. The "hills" should be prepared in the same manner as for lima beans, but set three feet apart, dropping five or six seeds in each hill. Cucumbers may be sown about the middle of May, and in succession, every three or four weeks, until July.

CURRANTS

The currant is useful both for dessert and for preserving purposes. An immense weight of fruit is obtained for the space it occupies, and the ease of its culture makes it common in every garden. The red and white varieties may be planted three or four feet apart each way, the black at four or five feet apart. Pruning is done in the fall by cutting off about a third of the young growth of the previous summer, and thinning out old shoots when the plants get too thick. All are trained in low bush form, the whites and reds usually from

three to four feet high and wide, the black four to six feet. They can also be grown trained against fences or walls like grape vines, and will, in such positions, attain eight or ten feet in height in five or six years from the time of planting, if the soil is deep and rich. . . .

An insect known as the currant worm is often very destructive. On its first appearance, if confined to a few leaves, these should be cut off, shoot and all, and destroyed. [Note to modern growers: Some varieties of currant are illegal in a number of states, as they were once thought to harbor disease fatal to white pines, an important timber crop. While this idea has pretty much been abandoned, the laws persist in some areas, so check with your local agricultural office.]

HERBS

Thyme, Sage, Basil, Sweet Marjoram, and Summer Savory are those in general use. The seeds of all should be sown in shallow drills, one foot apart, in May, and the plants will be fit for use in September and October.

HORSERADISH

For family use a few roots of this should be planted in some out-of-the-way corner of the vegetable garden. A dozen roots, once

planted, will usually give enough for a lifetime, as it increases and spreads so that there is never any danger of being without it. The trouble is, if it is once admitted in the garden, it is difficult to be rid of, if so desired.

LETTUCE

Lettuce should be sown in a hot-bed or greenhouse, if wanted early. Seeds sown there in February will give nice plants to set out in April, to mature in May; or, if it is sown in the open ground in April and planted out in May, it will mature in June, and so on through the summer season if successive crops are desired, as it only takes from five to six weeks to mature. . . . Although usually transplanted, the seed is also sown in rows, and the plants thinned out to twelve inches apart.

MELON

The cultivation of the melon is almost identical with that of the cucumber, to which reference may be made.

ONIONS

Onions are raised either from "sets," which are small dry onions grown the previous year, or from seeds. [Sets in today's parlance generally mean small sprouted plants which have been started from seed earlier in the same year.] When grown from the sets, they should be planted out as early in spring as the ground is dry enough to work. Plant them in rows one foot apart, with the sets three or four inches apart. When raised from sets, the onions can be used in the green state in June, or they will be ripened off by July. When raised from seeds, these are sown at about the same distance between the rows, and when the young plants are an inch or so high, they are thinned out to two or three inches apart. It is important that onion seed be sown very early. In this latitude it should be sown not later than the middle of April; for, if delayed until May, warm weather sets in and delays, or rather prolongs the growth until the fall, and often the bulbs will not ripen. We find that, unless the onion tops dry off and the bulbs ripen by August, they will hardly do so later.

PARSLEY

But a very small quantity of this is usually wanted in the family garden. Sow in shallow drills in April or May. A good plan is to sow in shallow boxes as much as may be needed. They can be placed wherever there is moderate light and no frost, in the kitchen window or similar place. By this means a fresh supply may be kept on hand in hard winter weather, when it is most desirable to have it, either for garnishing dishes or for other uses.

PEAS

For an early crop, peas should be one of the first things sown in the spring. We prefer to sow in double rows, which saves half the labor in stacking or bushing up, [i.e., tying, staking, or caging] and gives nearly the same crop to the row as if sown in single rows. Double rows are made at eight or nine inches apart, and four feet from other rows. Set a line, and draw the drills three or four inches deep with a hoe. The seed should be sown, as nearly as possible, an inch or so apart. In order to have a succession of crops of peas, they should be sown every two or three weeks until July. If successive crops are grown, an average quantity for family would be twelve quarts; if only first crops of early and late, from four to six quarts will be sufficient.

POTATOES

Potatoes are grown by planting the tubers, either cut or whole, it makes but little difference which. If large, cut them; if small leave them uncut. They are usually planted in drills three feet apart, and four or five inches deep. The ground should be prepared by first spreading in the drills a good coat of stable manure, say two inches deep, upon which are planted the tubers or sets, at distances of eight or ten inches apart. [Contrary to Henderson's advice, it would be best here not to use rotted manure, which could promote potato scab, but compost instead.] In a warm exposure, planting may be begun early, in April, and the crop will be fit for use in June.

RADISH

One of the first vegetables that we crave in spring is the radish, and it is so easy of culture that every family can have it fresh, crisp, and in abundance. A garden patch of a few feet square will give enough for an ordinary family. It is sown either in drills or broadcast, care being taken that the seed is not put in too thickly; from one to two inches apart, either in drill or broadcast, being the proper distance, as usually every seed germinates.

RASPBERRIES

To have the raspberry in perfection, the same preparation of soil is necessary as for the strawberry, only that, while, for the best results, the Strawberry bed must be perfectly clear of shade, the raspberries will do very well in a little shade; that is, in such a situation as will allow them one half or so of the sunlight. The canes or shoots of the raspberry are biennial; that is, the cane or shoot that is formed one season bears fruit the next season, and dies off after fruiting, giving place to the young cane that is to fruit the following season, and so on. The distances apart to plant the raspberry for garden culture may be, if in rows, four feet apart, with the plants two feet apart in the row; or, if in separate stools or hills, they may be set three feet each way; or, planted at distances of four feet apart, three plants may be put in each "hill," which will sooner secure a crop. They may be set in either fall or spring. If in the fall, a covering of four or five inches of dry leaves or litter should be spread over the roots to prevent them from getting too much frozen. Even when the plants are established and growing, it is necessary, in many cold sections, to bend down the canes and cover them with pine branches or some covering that will shield them from severe freezing. . . .

All the pruning that is necessary for the raspberry is to thin out the shoots in each hill to four or six. This is best done in the summer after the fruit is gathered, and at the same time the old canes that have borne the fruit should be cut out, so that the young shoots, coming forward to do duty next season, may have room to grow freely, and develop and ripen the wood. On rich soil these shoots are very vigorous, and, if left to grow unchecked, would reach seven to eight feet in height; but it is best to pinch out the tops of the young shoots when about six feet high. . . . When the leaves drop in fall, the canes may be shortened down a foot or so, which will complete the pruning-process.

To get the full benefit of all the fruit, it is very necessary to stake the raspberry. This may be done either by tying the canes of each plant separately to a stout stake, driven two feet or so into the ground, or, if grown in rows, they may be tied to wires running along the rows. The wires should be stretched between two stout posts, one at each end of the row, and three feet, more or less, above the ground, according to variety.

RHUBARB

Rhubarb may be planted in either fall or spring, using either plants raised from the seed, or sets, or sets obtained by division of the old roots, taking care to have a bud to each. Set at distances of three or four feet apart each way. The place where each plant is to be set should be dug eighteen inches deep and the same in width, and the soil mixed with two or three shovelfuls of well-rotted stable manure. Two dozen strong plants will be enough for the wants of an average family. If desired in winter or early spring, a few roots can be taken up and placed in a warm cellar or any such dark and warm place. The roots, if the cellar is dark, may be put in a box with earth around them, or if in a light cellar, they may be put in the bottom of a barrel with earth, and the top covered. The only care needed is to see that the roots do not get too dry, though water is rarely necessary when the plants are placed in a dark cellar. The useful portions are the long and thick leaf-stalks, and these, when forced, are much finer in flavor than when grown exposed to air and light in the open garden. The plants in the open ground should have the flower stalks cut away as they appear. In gathering do not cut the leaf stalks, as they will readily come away by a sidewise pull, and leave no remnant to decay.

SEA KALE

The seeds of sea kale should be sown in the greenhouse, or in a slight hot-bed in February or March, and when the plants are an inch or two in height, they should be potted in two or three-inch pots, and placed in a cold frame to harden, until sufficiently strong to be planted in the open ground. They should then be set out in rows three feet apart, with two feet between the plants, on land enriched as for any ordinary cabbage crop. If the plants and the soil in which they have been planted are both good, and cultivation has been properly attended to, by keeping the plants well hoed during the summer, they will have "crowns" strong enough to give a crop the next season. In the northern states it will be necessary to cover the rows with three or four inches of leaves, to protect the plants from frost. Sea kale is only fit for use when "blanched;" and to effect this, on the approach of spring the "crowns" should be covered with some light material, such as sand or leaf mold, to the depth of twelve to fifteen inches, so that the young shoots, being thus excluded from the light, will become blanched in growing through this covering. Sometimes cans made for this purpose, or even wooden boxes, are inverted over the plants, the object in each case being to exclude the light. If it is desired to force sea kale, or forward it earlier, the materials used to make hot-beds, leaves or stable manures, are heaped over the pots or cans in a sufficient quantity to generate the proper heat to forward the growth of the plants.

SPINACH

Spinach is a vegetable of easy culture. The seed may be sown either in spring or fall. If in the fall, the proper time is from the 10th to the 25th of September, in rows one foot apart. Sow rather thickly. Cover the plants with two or three inches of hay or leaves on the approach of severe frost in December. When sown in the fall, the crop, of course, is ready for use much earlier than when sown in the spring, as half the growth is made in the fall months. By the time the seed can be sown in the spring, the crop that has been wintered over will be coming into use. To fol-

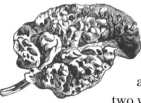

low the crop thus wintered, seeds should be sown in the same manner in the spring, as early as the soil can be worked, and another sowing may be made two weeks later.

STRAWBERRIES

Of all the small fruits none stand so high in general favor as the strawberry. Its culture is simple; and as it grows freely in almost any soil, adapting itself to the climate of the extreme South as well as to our most Northern States, no garden of any pretensions should be without it. If a choice soil can be had, nothing is so suitable as a deep, rich, but rather sandy loam, though it will yield returns sufficient to warrant its cultivation on any soil, from almost pure sand to clay, provided it is drained naturally or artificially. In all soils, deep spading or plowing is essential to the production of fine crops; and this should not be less than a

foot, and if eighteen inches, all the better. A coat of thoroughly rotted stable manure, at least three inches in thickness, should be dug in and well mixed with the soil to a depth of six or nine inches. . . . Where muck from the swamps or leaf mold from the woods can be obtained, twenty bushels of either of these mixed with one bushel of ashes will make an excellent fertilizer for strawberries, and may be spread on as thickly as stable manure, and on sandy soils is probably better.

Strawberries may be planted either in the fall or spring. If the plants are to be set in the fall, it should not be done before the middle of September. This, of course, refers to the plants from runners taken up from the bed in the usual manner; and there is nothing gained in time over planting the next spring, as the plant must grow for one season before it can bear a full crop of fruit. In private gardens it is much better to have the plants layered in pots, as they may then be set at almost any time. These pots may be from two to three inches in diameter. When a lot of strawberry plants are wanted for a new bed, all that is necessary to do is to fill these small pots with soil, and "plunge" or plant the pot just to the surface level, placing the unrooted "runner" of the strawberry plant on the top of the soil in the flower pot, and laying a small stone or clod on it to keep it in place.

There is one very important point in strawberry culture that should never be neglected; and that is that the beds be entirely covered with hay, straw, or leaves, to the depth of three or four inches. This covering should not be put on however, before the approach of severe weather. . . . This covering should not be taken off in spring. It is only necessary to go over the beds as soon as growth begins, and pull the covering back from the plants just sufficient to expose the crown, allowing all to remain on the bed. This covering serves several purposes. It keeps the roots warm until the plants start to grow; it keeps the fruit clean when ripe; it prevents the growth of weeds, and finally, acts as a mulch to keep the soil from drying in hot weather.

TOMATO

The tomato will grow anywhere, and almost under any circumstances, provided always that it has the necessary high temperature. It is essentially a plant of the tropics, and need never be sown in a hot-bed here before March, or planted in the open ground before the middle of May. When grown in private gardens, the tomato should always be provided with some sort of trellis or be tacked up against a fence or wall. By this treatment, not only will a heavier crop be obtained, but the flavor will be better. When the fruit rests on the ground it has often an inferior flavor, particularly when eaten raw, and is also more apt to decay. A few dozen plants usually suffice for an ordinary family; and if there are no hot-beds or other glass arrangements on hand, the plants had better be purchased, as they are sold cheaply everywhere.

TURNIP

The turnip, if wanted for an early crop, is sown in early spring, as directed for beets. . . . If for winter or fall use, sowing should be deferred until July or August. The rutabaga or swedes are sown in July and the earlier winter sorts, such as Yellow Globe or Flat Dutch, in August.

Pears were one of the most popular fruits on the tables of Point Ellice, at least if the O'Reilly letters are any indication. While apples, cherries, and plums were also grown throughout the garden, pears are mentioned frequently, and no wonder. Of all the fruit trees imported to the New World, only the apple has a longer history, or was held in higher regard on the Victorian dinner table.

The common pear, *Pyrus communis*, had been cultivated in western Asia since before the time of the Greeks, and was carried into Europe by the Romans. Pears crossbreed easily, and two groups were already known and named by the Roman naturalist Pliny the Elder: the "proud" pears, so-called because they ripened early and wouldn't "deign" to be kept; and the "winter" pears, which were used for cooking and baking. According to Pliny, however, all these Roman pears had one not-so-boastful thing in common, "pears without exception are quite tough, unless they are well boiled or baked."

It was not until the eighteenth century that the tender, luscious pears the O'Reillys so loved were developed. For these delicacies, like many others, they were in debt to the French and the Belgians, who were, quite simply, crazy about pears. Pears were considered the quintessential dessert for the autumn and early winter table on the continent, and sizable amounts of time and effort had been dedicated to producing buttery, aromatic fruit that would literally melt in your mouth. The names of some of these exquisite varieties still bear witness to this flurry of Gallic breeding: 'Beurré Bosc,' 'Doyenne du Comice,' 'Rouselette de Riems' and 'Belle Angevine' to name a few. Thousands of luscious new varieties were bred, and the pear seemed poised finally to overtake its age-old rival the apple as the king of fruits.

Pears had come to American shores with the first colonists, and with the arrival of each new European variety, they were more and more enthusiastically received. Large orchards were established in areas congenial to its habit, especially in New England, and the pear's future seemed bright in the New World. Then disaster struck, for hiding in North American forests was an until-then-unknown bacterium, *Erwinia amylovara* (commonly called fire blight), which proved deadly to this defenseless European import. Fire blight didn't just weaken or maim the pear, it attacked and killed entire trees.

PEARS

Roots, trunks, limbs, flowers, fruit, and leaves were left a blackened mass of withered foliage, sometimes taking only a matter of weeks to destroy an established tree.

To make matters worse, the occurrence of fire blight was also erratic, lulling growers into a disastrous sense of false security. Sometimes decades passed without a major outbreak, and then rapid and total decimation would occur. There was, and still is, no known cure. The best that could be hoped for was that in cutting off the infected branch or portion of the tree, the remainder could be spared if done early enough. While this treatment could be successful on a limited domestic scale like that practiced by the O'Reillys, for commercial orchards with their large monocultures it proved almost impossible, and entire stands of pears were often wiped out in a single season, especially east of the Mississippi where the disease was most rampant. Needless to say, the cultivation of pears went into steep decline, and it looked as if the fruit would be relegated to the marginalia of North American gardening history.

But to the rescue came the pear's Oriental cousin, *Pyrus serotina*, which was imported to North America early in the nineteenth century. Commonly called the sand pear, because the flesh contained numerous "sandy" or gritty cells which gave the fruit a grainy texture when compared to the buttery smooth European pears, this Asian native did prove to have one shining characteristic. It was more or less resistant to fire blight. Planted in areas where fire blight was a problem, the sand pear soon interbred with its European cousin and produced a number of good-tasting, disease-resistant varieties. These in turn produced a host of even better tasting, hardy cultivars. Thanks to the introduction of this disease resistance, and the discovery that fire blight was less of concern in the dry valleys of the far West and the Pacific Northwest, commercial pear production in North America was able to recover, albeit generally limited to a handful of varieties selected more for shipping and shelf life than for taste.

Fortunately, the average home gardener isn't limited by these same constraints, and it's high time that some of these wonderful varieties of pears never found in the market be restored to their rightful place in the garden. There are now dozens of cultivars resistant to blight, and even many of the older, more susceptible varieties may be grown successfully in many parts of the country by the average gardener. Which variety you choose, of course, depends on your taste and planned usage. There are pears bred specifically for eating by hand, for culinary purposes, or for the dessert table—all delicious additions to the modern garden.

CHAPTER VII
THE WOODLAND GARDEN

Nature Versus Nurture • Creating Opportunities • Special Considerations
Plants for the Wild Garden • Fern Mania • PLANTS WITH A PAST: Giant Sequoia

One of the most interesting, and unfortunately, one of the least-documented parts of the Point Ellice garden is the northern portion of the lot between the house and Selkirk Water. Bounded today by a circular promenade that leads down from the croquet lawn, across the sloping bank along the shore, and back up to the rear of the house, this section of the garden had almost completely returned to wilderness by the time the house was acquired by the Province of British Columbia in the early 1970s. In fact, so untamed was this area that initially the conservation staff presumed the space had never been part of the garden at all. Subsequent investigations, however, discovered the remains of a walkway network; certain large nonnative trees, such as horse chestnut, copper beech, and linden; as well as other nonnative shrubs—conclusive evidence that this area had probably once been the O'Reillys' woodland garden, a common feature in late Victorian landscapes.

Nature Versus Nurture

The rise of these woodland gardens was yet another product of the indefatigable efforts of William Robinson to reshape the way Victorians gardened. As a natural extension of his campaign against bedding out and "artificial manipulations" of flowers (see Chapter III) Robinson promoted the concept of the wild or natural garden space as the perfect means to showcase many less common, underused flowers and shrubs in a more relaxed, carefree manner. He argued, with considerable justification, that the energy and expense devoted to raising nonhardy plants year after year was a time-consuming and costly effort whose energy might better be focused elsewhere.

To most people, a pretty plant in a free state is more attractive than any garden denizen. It is taking care of itself, and moreover, it is usually surrounded by some degree of graceful wild spray—the green above, and the moss and brambles and grass around. . . . Numbers of plants of the highest order and fragrance, and clothed with pleasant associations, may be seen perfectly at home in the spaces now devoted to rank grass and weeds, and by wooded walks in our shrubberies and ornamental plantations. . . . We may have more of the varied beauty of hardy flowers than the most ardent admirer of the old style of garden ever dreams of, by naturalizing innumerable beautiful natives of many regions of the earth in our woods and copses, rougher parts of pleasure grounds, and in unoccupied places in almost every kind of garden.

—WILLIAM ROBINSON,
The Wild Garden

A winding path bordered with ivy wanders into the woodland garden.

Robinson continues by listing additional reasons why one should undertake creating a more natural landscape:

- Hundreds of the finest hardy flowers will thrive much better in rough and wild places than ever they did in the flower border.

- These same plants will also look infinitely better than ever they did in gardens when allowed to grow in a natural state and follow their own predilections.

- Wild gardens keep a much neater experience throughout the entire year than do traditional gardening areas such as perennial or annual borders. In the wild garden, plants can bloom, and then fade back unmolested into a natural back ground, to be replaced by other flowers and points of interest in seasonal succession.

- One can grow all sorts of charming plants not generally considered sufficiently ornamental for the border, as well as their reverse counterparts: those plants that have spectacular flowers or foliage, but whose rambunctious growing habits make them unsuitable for the confines of more formalized growing areas.

- The wild garden also solves the problem of how to best use spring bulbs: In a woodland space they can be planted without the worry of faded blooms or decaying foliage.

And finally, and perhaps most importantly for Point Ellice:

> The great merit of permanence belongs to this delightful phase of gardening. Select a wild rough slope, and embellish it with the handsomest and hardiest climbing plants. . . . Arranged with some judgment at first, such a colony might be left to take care of itself; time would but add to its attractions, and the happy owner might go away for years, and find it beautiful on his return.
>
> —WILLIAM ROBINSON,
> *The Wild Garden*

It's hard to know, after the passage of more than 130 years, exactly what the O'Reillys had in mind when they laid out their woodland garden. The "great merit of permanence" Robinson ascribes to such gardens was to be measured in single years, not decades or centuries. What seems clear, however, given the fragmentary evidence of the garden that is left to us today, is that Peter O'Reilly and his family intended a woodland landscape not unlike the one Robinson describes. Certainly, such a garden would have then been at the very height of fashion, something quite important to the socially sensitive O'Reillys. But even more significant, this particular style of garden, dedicated to reuniting the man-made landscape with that of nature, couldn't have been more appropriate to the setting of Point Ellice House. Carved out of virgin forest just a few years before, much of the lot and adja-

An arbor beckons the modern visitor to explore the woodland garden.

cent land near the shoreline was still scattered with large trees and copses of woods and bramble, a situation many modern owners of newly created lots can readily identify with. Robinson's wild-garden style was perfect for these rougher portions of Point Ellice, and is equally valid for similar situations today.

Creating Opportunities

So how do you go about making a wild garden? As with any other kind of garden, selecting the proper site is the first order of business, although with wild gardens, the process is a bit different. Unlike most other types of landscape design that generally start with a fairly blank slate, the wild garden is best created around a feature already existing in the landscape. Places that would not normally be considered suitable for more standardized planting schemes are often perfect for wild gardens. Here are just a few of the possibilities:

- the banks of a small stream planted with moisture-loving species

- the margin of a meadow turned into a garden of spring bulbs and wildflowers

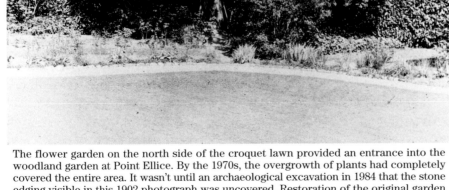

The flower garden on the north side of the croquet lawn provided an entrance into the woodland garden at Point Ellice. By the 1970s, the overgrowth of plants had completely covered the entire area. It wasn't until an archaeological excavation in 1984 that the stone edging visible in this 1902 photograph was uncovered. Restoration of the original garden path, edging, and flower garden took place between 1988 and 1989.

- the area under a canopy of large trees underplanted with spring bulbs and shade-loving plants

- a rocky outcrop or stone wall interspersed with alpines and other plants that thrive in poor soil

- a small pond ornamented with waterlilies

- a small woodland underplanted with azaleas, rhododendrons, and climbing plants like wisteria or Virginia creeper

Special Considerations

Whatever opportunity presents itself in your yard, it is important to make sure that visibility and access are addressed sensitively. Unless you spend a great deal of time outdoors, for instance, you probably wouldn't want to place your garden so far off the beaten path that your visits would be infrequent—especially since wild gardens rarely put on spectacular single displays, and yield their pleasures slowly over time. On the other hand, removing large numbers of trees to open up a view to your intended site or otherwise radically altering existing conditions specifically to create a "wilderness" will often defeat the purpose of this type of garden entirely. While it is in fact possible to "construct" such "natural" areas where they didn't exist before, unless the design is very cleverly conceived and undertaken, the effect generally looks forced and contrived.

The same caveat holds true for methods of access. Because of the reserved nature of the wild garden, its delights are often best appreciated close at hand, requiring some type of path or walkway that allows you to move through the space. Rustic paths, like the gravel ones found at Point Ellice, or walks formed simply of packed earth or wood chips, are de rigueur. Obviously anything that looks too manmade or artificial would seem very much out of place.

After you have selected a suitable spot for your garden, the next consideration is to analyze thoroughly your site's growing conditions. Different areas will present distinct challenges to be overcome, as well as distinct advantages to be enjoyed. An area near a stream, for instance, will undoubtedly be quite moist a large part of the year, limiting your plant selection to those that thrive in damp or boggy soils. On the upside, however, the warmth created by constantly flowing water will often permit you to select species not normally hardy in your growing zone. In fact in such places you can often extend your selection range upward a full growing zone or more.

The margins of woodland garden and the more cultivated portions of the general landscape make excellent areas for growing larger-scale shrubs and perennials like these.

Woodland sites, like the garden at Point Ellice, present special challenges and opportunities. Anyone who has taken shelter under the canopy of a large tree during a sudden summer shower knows how effective heavy foliage can be in deflecting water. So much so, in fact, that the ground under many large trees is usually considerably drier than that just beyond the leaf cover. Another factor is the rapacious root system of large trees. Species like the Norway maple send out an almost impenetrable system of fine, fibrous roots that make digging any more than a few inches deep a nightmare. This same root network also effectively drains the soil of any nutrients with which it comes in contact. Once again, this is not an impossible situation. In the natural woodlands many plants thrive in such situations, and supplemental water and soil enhancement can go a long way in getting new plantings established in woodland settings. The key is simply to make sure you choose plants that will do well in whatever conditions currently exist at your site. Unlike most other gardening styles in which the gardener substantially alters or enhances nature to conform to his or her whim, in the woodland garden, success is only achieved when the gardener bends to the will of Mother Nature.

PLANTS FOR THE WILD GARDEN

William Robinson, the great Victorian horti-culturist and garden writer, recommended the following annuals, perennials, and vines as suitable in form and habit for the wild garden. They are, however, quite diverse in terms of growing requirements, and it would behoove the gardener to make sure that each plant's requirements conform to the conditions found at their particular site before purchase and planting.

BOTANICAL NAME	COMMON NAME
Acanthus mollis	Acanthus
Aconitum spp.	Monkshood
Aconitum spp.	Aconite
Anemonella thalictroides	Windflower
Antirrhinum spp.	Snapdragon
Aquilegia spp.	Columbine
Arenaria spp.	Sandwort
Asphodeline lutea	Jacob's Rod
Aubrietia deltoidea	Purple Rock Cress
Borago officinalis	Borage
Campanula spp.	Bellflower
Centaurea cyanus	Cornflower
Chrysanthemum leucanthemum	Ox-eye Daisy
Clematis spp.	Clematis
Colchicum autumnale	Meadow Saffron
Coronilla varia	Crown vetch
Crocus spp.	Crocus
Cyclamen spp.	Cyclamen
Cytisus spp.	Broom
Digitalis spp.	Foxglove
Doronicum spp.	Leopard's bane
Echinops spp.	Globe thistles
Erica spp.	Heath
Eryngium spp.	Sea Holly
Erysimum spp.	Wallflower
Erythronium spp.	Dogtooth Violet
Ferula communis	Giant Fennel
Fritillaria Meleagris	Snake's-head
Galanthus	Snowdrop
Geranium endressi	Cranesbill
Geum montanum	Mountain Aven

BOTANICAL NAME	COMMON NAME
Helianthemum spp.	Sun Rose
Helianthus spp.	Sunflower (Perennial)
Hemerocallis spp.	Daylily
Hepatica spp.	Hepatica
Heracleum lanatum	Cow Parsnip
Hosta spp.	Hosta
Hypericum spp.	St. John's Wort
Iris spp.	Iris
Lathyrus grandiflorus	Sweet pea
Lavandula spp.	Lavender
Leucojum spp.	Snowflakes
Lilium philadelphicum	Wood Lily
Lilium spp.	Lily
Lonicera spp.	Honeysuckle
Lunaria annua	Honesty
Lupinus spp.	Lupine
Maianthemum canadense	Lily of the valley
Malva spp.	Mallow
Mimulus spp.	Monkeyflower
Monarda didyma	Bee Balm
Muscari spp.	Grape Hyacinth
Myosotis scorpioides	Forget-me-not
Narcissus spp.	Daffodil
Nymphaea spp.	Water Lily
Oenothera biennis	Evening Primrose
Omphalodes verna	Creeping Navel-seed
Ononis spp.	Rest-harrow
Onopordum spp.	Cotton Thistle
Ornithogalum spp.	Star of Bethlehem
Paeonia spp.	Peony

BOTANICAL NAME	COMMON NAME
Papaver spp.	Poppy
Paradisea liliastrum	St. Bruno's Lily
Parthenocissus quinquefolia	Virginia Creeper
Petasites fragrans	Winter Heliotrope
Phlox spp.	Phlox
Phytolacca americana	Virginia Poke
Polygonatum spp.	Solomon's Seal
Polygonum convolvulus	Bindweed
Polygonum spp.	Knotwort
Pulmonaria angustifolia	Lungwort
Rosa spp.	Rose
Sanguinaria canadensis	Bloodroot
Scabiosa spp.	Scabious
Scilla spp.	Squill
Sedum spp.	Stonecrop
Sempervivum spp.	Houseleek
Silphium laciniatum	Compass Plant
Solidago canadensis	Goldenrod
Spiraea latifolia	Meadowsweet
Stellaria media	Starwort
Symphytum officinale	Comfrey
Thalictrum spp.	Meadow Rue
Thymus spp.	Thyme
Trollius spp.	Globeflower
Tulipa spp.	Tulip
Vancouveria hexandra	Barrenwort
Verbascum spp.	Mullein
Vinca spp.	Periwinkle
Viola spp.	Violet
Wisteria spp.	Wisteria

Fern Mania

The Victorian era was probably host to more gardening fads than any other period in modern history. Driven by technological innovations that suddenly made growing previously difficult species relatively easy and inexpensive, popular demand for such novelties as variegated plants, exotic annuals, and orchids all reached unheard-of heights during the last half of the nineteenth century. Perhaps none of these crazes, however, was as widespread, or lasted longer, or had more impact on society as a whole, than the almost unbelievable passion for ferns that dominated British and American gardening circles until World War I.

It all started innocently enough. Previous to 1840, ferns were simply considered pleasant additions to woodland and wild settings, with little or no economical value, other than occasional medicinal use. Then in 1842 there appeared a little book by Nathaniel Ward, *On the Growth of Plants in Closely Glazed Cases*, which showed for the first time how plants could be easily grown indoors, where before most had quickly perished (see Chapter V). Ward's solution, the terrarium, or Wardian case, as it quickly came to be known, proved the ideal place for growing previously temperamental plants never before seen in the parlor.

Chief among these were the newly rediscovered ferns, which up to this time had been almost impossible to grow indoors. Their delicate tracery and interesting habits and history perfectly matched the Victorian taste for the new and unique, and multiple books on ferns and fern culture quickly appeared. More than four hundred were published in Britain alone before 1900.

Within a few years, miniature glassed woodlands loaded with ferns began to grace drawing rooms of taste all over Europe and America, and outdoor ferneries, as specialty fern gardens were then called, became a standard feature in any garden with pretensions to the name.

But where to get one's ferns? Few nurseries of the day carried them, and even fewer understood much about the fern's primitive reproductive cycle. One of the oldest plant species on earth, *Pteridophyta* (to use the fern's proper name) employ a complicated two-stage reproductive system involving spores instead of seeds. The obvious answer to the supply dilemma was simply to collect ferns in the wild. Fern hunting became a social event, especially among the ladies, and daylong parties complete with refreshments were organized for the purpose. Basket loads of ferns were gathered not only for transplanting to indoor and outdoor gardens, but for decorative purposes. Fern fronds were highly sought-after table decora-

KATHLEEN TO PAPA—NEW YEAR'S DAY, 1878

Alice Ward went with me to gather some ferns for Mama's dinner party.

tions, and were often dried and preserved through pressing for use in innumerable creative ways. Fern motifs became popular in prints, linens, pottery, and even ironwork.

Gardeners with ample time and leisure began to develop large fern collections, and avid collectors often organized special expeditions, often utilizing truly clever means to secure a particular prize, as this excerpt from *British Ferns and Their Varieties*, 1910, shows:

> Of course it occasionally happens that the successful hunter is confronted with difficulties which will tax his inventive powers to overcome . . . a very desirable hart's tongue was noticed just over the arch spanning a Devonshire stream, and only just within reach of a trowel lashed to a stick. If dislodged it would inevitably fall into the rapid stream below and be lost. The problem was solved by the fortunate presence of an umbrella, which being opened and suspended under the arch by a string, eventually received the prize when dislodged. A second similar bridge difficulty with a variety of *Polypodium vulgare* was met differently: the umbrella could not be used as the wall was sheer, but by means of a loose slip knot of string, the fronds were lassoed, and when the root was dislodged, the plant was drawn up and bagged. . . .

By the late 1800s, in fact, so great had the demand for ferns grown and so popular the hobby of gathering them that certain varieties began to be locally extinct in many parts of Britain and America. Collecting in the wild is now illegal in many countries and, given the availability of ferns in commerce today, should in any case be discouraged. Fortunately, the huge demand for ferns led to the establishment of societies dedicated to the preservation and cultivation of the genus, which in turn helped to establish centers for commercial fern production. However, the wilds of Victorian British Columbia around Point Ellice House, with its moist damp climate so perfect for growing ferns, never suffered a supply problem. Whatever ferns the O'Reillys required were simply collected from the forests and fields around them, and almost certainly ferns played an important part in their woodland garden.

Fortunately for the rest of us, ferns are remarkably easy to grow outside of the Pacific Northwest, and, given the adaptability of the genus, can be used in most areas of North America. It is a common misconception that ferns are tender, and always require shady, boggy sites; while there certainly are ferns that need such conditions, there are hosts of others that are perfectly hardy and thrive in dry shade, even in rocky, sun-drenched surroundings. In short, there is probably a fern for more spots in your garden than you ever thought possible. Ferns are particularly at home, however, in partially shaded tree-covered settings, where their loose, relaxed spirit makes them the quintessential woodland plant.

While the fern family is huge, some broad cultural generalizations can be made: Although most ferns are generally indifferent to pH considerations, they do require a fairly rich soil that while moist is also well drained. The humusy leaf mold of a wooded bank is ideal for many ferns, which is why they are excellent candidates for the wild garden. Most ferns prefer some shade and don't do terribly well in very windy spots since their fronds are surprisingly delicate and damage easily.

The fern family is so large that it's often difficult for the beginner to know where to start; in general most members of the large *Dryopteris* and *Poly-stichum* families are good choices. Here are some specific suggestions for ferns that are reasonably rugged and do well in challenging conditions, like those found in a woodland garden.

BOTANICAL NAME	COMMON NAME	ZONE
D. carthusiana	Spinulose wood fern	Zone 3
D. erythrosora	Autumn fern	Zone 6
D. felix-mas	Male fern	Zone 4
D. formosa	Formosan fern	Zone 7
D. intermedia	Fancy wood fern	Zone 4
D. marginalis	Marginal wood fern	Zone 4
D. x remota		Zone 5
P. acrostichoides	Christmas fern	Zone 3
P. braunii	Braun's holly fern	Zone 4
P. munitum	Western sword fern	Zone 6
P. setiferum cus.	Soft shield fern	Zone 5

One final note: Although most ferns are very well behaved, generally staying in the places where you put them and slowly expanding into larger clumps, some ferns can become quite invasive. Before making any selections for your garden, it's best to ask an expert or consult a good book—one of the best of recent years is Martin Rickard's *The Plantfinder's Guide to Garden Ferns*.

CAROLINE TO PETER—20 MAY 1871

Today I have worked like a horse in the garden. The weeds are dreadful and the ground is so hard to dig! I have cleared and dug up the ground around the wellingtonia gigantea and am to sow mignonette. I think the garden will look very pretty.... I think how I do wish, dear one, that you were here and that I could hope that you would return in time to see it in its beauty, but alas there is no hope.

One of the largest plants at Point Ellice is still really just a baby, the huge *Sequoiadendron giganteum* located in the woodland garden north of the croquet lawn. Planted by Peter O'Reilly before 1871 and now over 120 years old, this towering giant could potentially grow another 200 feet, and given a good run, live a thousand more years.

The Giant Sequoia and its close cousin Redwood belong to one of the oldest tree species in the world, which before the last Ice Age once dominated the forests of North America and Europe. Then came the glaciers, and these huge forests were cut off, swept away, and destroyed by the advancing ice sheets. Of the many thousands of square miles the trees formerly occupied, only a few scattered stands remained along the protected coasts of California to greet the first Europeans. Immediately recognized for its rarity, the Giant Sequoia became the subject of some patriotic name pulling during the cultural and economic competition in the early 1850s between imperial Britain and the rapidly expanding United States. The tree was first christened *Sequoia gigantea*, a name that unfortunately had already been assigned to the Redwood a few years previously. Then in 1855, the pro-British *S. Wellingtonia* was suggested, to honor the

GIANT SEQUOIA

English hero of that name; the Americans, not to be outdone, then proposed *Taxodium washingtonianum*, or *Washingtoniana californica*, depending on the tree's final species assignment. (It was unclear at the time to exactly which botanical family the tree belonged.) The debate continued well into the early twentieth century, with different parties each using different names. The patriotic O'Reillys, of course, always used the British version. Finally, *Sequoiadendron giganteum* was officially decided upon, although old habits die hard and many people still call the tree a Wellingtonia.

By whatever name, the Giant Sequoia still looks as big, and if you have ample space and a fairly mild climate, it makes a fantastic specimen tree. *S. giganteum* is actually a fairly rapid grower in its early years, with lush bluish-green needles and rich reddish bark. As the tree ages, it gradually loses its lower branches, giving it a slim, raised pyramidal shape at maturity. Although a giant in the wild, the tree generally remains smaller in cultivation: 60 to 100 feet tall. Supposedly hardy to Zones 6 to 8, there is some evidence that the tree can withstand much more severe cold. Water, however, is another matter. Native to the moist coastal forests, this remarkable link to our prehistoric past cannot tolerate extended periods of drought.

CHAPTER VIII
HOW SCIENCE CAME TO THE GARDEN,
- OR -
HOW WE KNOW WHAT WE KNOW ABOUT THE POINT ELLICE LANDSCAPE

Piecing Together a Garden's Past • Garden Archaeology at Point Ellice
Small Beginnings • Making Connections • A Flower of Their Own: The Point Ellice Hollyhocks
The Greenhouse Takes Shape • Dig-Less Archaeology • PLANTS WITH A PAST: Ivy

Piecing Together a Garden's Past

One early spring day, Peter O'Reilly, home for a brief few weeks between business trips, was anxious to get the kitchen garden planted. The seedlings, started by Tom, one of the Chinese servants, had sprouted rapidly in the greenhouse. Now, many of the tiny plants had been moved to the kitchen garden where they were hardening off in the cold frames, and it was time to map out exactly where each crop would eventually go. Walking out of the greenhouse, gravel crunching underfoot, he ambled his way east along the path, scribbling precise planting instructions as he went. After completing his circuit of the garden, he returned to the greenhouse along a walkway that skirted the garden's most westerly edge and ended at the greenhouse door. Although this imaginary

scenario may sound simple enough, it raises a question that has plagued archaeologists and Point Ellice historians for years. What did that western path consist of and where exactly did it run?

While this historical puzzle might not compare with such archaeological quests as the search for King Tut's tomb, ignorance of simple details like these hampers efforts to reconstruct accurately the Point Ellice property and complete the history of the O'Reilly family. One of the archaeologists who sought an answer was Sharon Keen, who spent a wet spring in 1994 patiently probing the ground outside the greenhouse door with a foot-long $1/2$-inch-wide metal spike. Because other paths around the garden had been discovered relatively close to the surface, Keen theorized that she could find the missing walkway in question by detecting a change in resistance between the rich soil where

a century-old garden ended and a sturdier path of brick, gravel, or even packed sand began. But Keen couldn't find it. At least two other archaeologists also probed, dug, or surveyed the garden with sophisticated electronic tools; but in the end, the exact route of the path remains a mystery to this day. Perhaps the original, made of packed earth, dissolved over time into the surrounding gardens. Maybe it was a gravel or brick path and at some time the material was simply removed during an earlier garden renovation. We may never know for sure.

Why be concerned about garden details like these? Besides providing essential information about the house and its setting, the landscape can often yield many insights into the times of its construction and the people who built and tended it. For example, a house that is discovered to have had a large and ornate garden most likely would have been tended by servants, giving a good indication of the family's wealth. A smaller than normal kitchen garden might indicate that there were few mouths to feed in a household. The uncovering of a large plot for staple crops such as root vegetables, which were easily stored in abundance, might suggest a family of limited means with a need to keep its economic feet firmly planted. Gar-

Top: The newly finished portion of the kitchen garden planted with heirloom flowers and vegetables. The path to the left of the picture runs to where the O'Reilly greenhouse once stood. The cold frames were located immediately to the greenhouse's right.

Above: Although unprepossessing, tiny plant fragments such as these can give archaeologists valuable insights into what once grew where.

den research can even provide clues to ethnicity: A predominance of cabbage or soup potatoes might

Opposite—top left: The garden's restoration commences with a tape measure and soil probes as archaeologists begin to determine the original extent of the kitchen garden pathways. *Top right:* The kitchen garden excavation begins. The white picket fencing just visible in the background was replaced soon afterward, reproducing the original design chosen by Peter and Caroline. To the right of this photograph, where large hollies now stand, the O'Reillys and Drakes had installed trellis fencing along the property line forming a barrier between their respective gardens. On the O'Reilly side of the fence, archaeologists found some indications of curving brick pathways, and period documents indicate that the O'Reillys had planted a variety of roses there. *Bottom right:* The north-south kitchen garden path under construction. Original bricks, gravel, and rock used for the O'Reilly garden paths were discovered after turf laid in the 1950s and 60s had been carefully removed. *Bottom left:* The partially reconstructed kitchen garden in the mid-1990s. Extensive research and excavation revealed the location of most of the major pathways, but the internal layout of the original garden is still a mystery, as is that of the area (currently lawn) just to the right in the photograph. Research by the authors, as well as reinterpreted period photographic evidence, suggests that the kitchen garden originally encompassed this area as well.

Garden archaeology often begins long before the digging even starts. Here, period photos helped solve a mystery. The photo above clearly showed a lovely garden, but where exactly had it been located on the property? By carefully counting the cobbles and comparing the shapes and sizes in these two views, it was demonstrated conclusively that this garden is in fact the extension of the garden shown below, running along the north side of the croquet lawn.

indicate the arrival of the first German family in a traditionally Italian region otherwise replete with tomato- and oregano-filled gardens.

Garden Archaeology at Point Ellice

Unfortunately, garden archaeology often ranks low on the list of priorities at many historical sites in North America. The reasons are numerous. Non-profit organizations like these almost always have limited funds and tend to use them to restore buildings, where research results are more quickly evident and generally provide greater tourist draws. At other sites, the landscape has often been subdivided or built over so heavily that restoration is impossible. Perhaps the most important reason, however, why garden research lags behind that of interiors is that curators and administrators do not always recognize the vital role the landscape can play in illuminating the life and times of the people who created them.

Even Point Ellice House was not immune to this bias, at least initially. Despite the obvious significance of the gardens to the O'Reilly family, fiscal priorities of the initial years were almost entirely focused on the structures. As more became known about the quality and potential of the garden, however, attention began to shift to the outdoors as well, and garden experts were called in. While the scope of the first projects was limited, the work soon attracted the attention of local residents, eager to protect the treasured Victorian beauty, as well as outside garden historians who recognized the uniqueness of the restoration opportunity. Finally, more funds became available and ever since,

working under very tight budgets, archaeologists and historians have slowly revealed and restored the complexities of the Point Ellice landscape.

Garden archaeology, though, can be a perplexing pursuit. The problem, of course, is the nature of gardens themselves: Unlike palaces or temples, they are ephemeral by design. Gardens change over the years at the whim of nature or the gardener. How many times have you rotated your crops or moved around your plot to take advantage of more sun or to thwart a particular pest? At Point Ellice, the kitchen garden, for example, went through several incarnations. Purely practical vegetables during Peter's tenure gave way to more and more flowers under Kathleen's stewardship, and finally, after her death, Peter O'Reilly's grandson John eliminated the kitchen garden entirely by planting a lawn over it. Other abandoned parts of the landscape succumbed quickly to weeds, ivy, and other fast-growing plants, making the original design hard to decipher.

Small Beginnings

Garden archaeology, as with all good archaeology, begins not with digging through dirt, but searching through old books, papers, letters, and other writers' records. Documentation such as town maps, surveys, and even old insurance policies provide clues to landscape designs, outbuildings, fence lines, and plot locations. Often, as at Point Ellice, notes from the landowners describe the gardens in detail. Letters to family members tout the success of a remarkable flower or mourn the failure of a poor harvest of corn. A file or shoebox full of receipts may reveal the purchase of specialized garden supplies such as an expensive new lawn mower, suggesting the existence of a large lawn, or a shipment of bricks for a new walk or wall. Before an archaeologist digs, paper trails such as these help the researcher form a strong theory about what the landscape may have looked like, and serve to focus the excavation's potential. After thorough research, the painstaking process of digging begins. Slowly, the archaeologists start looking for the remains of hardscape structures such as fences, pathways, or wells. Different colors of soil show where pathways ended and a growing bed began. Pollen analysis can sometimes identify which specific plants were grown and when. Researchers can also search for microscopic fossil-like remains called phytoliths. Invisible to the naked eye, phytoliths are pieces of silica that form when the minerals in water crystallize and form a cast of the plant cell wall. Surviving in the soil even after a plant decomposes or is burned, phytoliths can often reveal what species grew in a particular area or garden.

Sometimes living plants hold the key to a garden's past. While examining a row of trees that had grown up near the carriage way at Point Ellice, garden historian Cyril Hume noticed that the plants bore marks, such as codominant leaders and wide crotches in the branches, that indicated they had been heavily pruned at one point. Looking at old photographs, Hume realized that these gangly trees had been planted in the 1880s, and were originally pruned into hedges. After carefully rooting cuttings from the original specimens, the trees were removed and new hedges were replanted, restoring the appearance of the carriage way to one that would have been familiar to Peter and Caroline as they arrived at and departed from Point Ellice.

Making Connections

As in the case of the hedges along the drive, most discoveries made at Point Ellice, or any other historical site for that matter, usually involve a convergence of seemingly divergent bits of evidence. For example, researchers found a garden catalog at Point Ellice with the order form missing and a notation in Peter's diary that he had sent money to the company for flowers. Then little scribbled tick marks were discovered next to some of the flower descriptions, but there was no sure indication of which ones had been ordered. That answer came in the form of a journal entry made around the same time by Kathleen in which she tells of planting gladiolas, with notes indicating exactly where she planted them. With all three pieces of evidence in hand, historians at Point Ellice were able not only to determine exactly which species of gladiola had been purchased, but also where each had grown—an amazing bit of historical detective work.

The plants you see at the Point Ellice garden today are all ranked according to historical significance. Plants in the first class are especially precious because these are original specimens, planted by the O'Reillys and still growing where they did when the O'Reillys inhabited the premises. Next, in order of importance, are the historical replacements. Based on a confluence of evidence, these plantings, such as Katherine's

A FLOWER OF THEIR OWN: THE POINT ELLICE HOLLYHOCKS

Sometimes researchers dig for years only to discover a single new historical fact. Other times, Mother Nature thrusts revelations into their faces.

When garden historian Cyril Hume arrived at Point Ellice, the north end of the tennis lawn, which abutted the woodland garden and its pathways, was shrouded with vegetation. As Hume cut away the growth, he was able to discern the limits of paths and borders.

As these cleared areas were once again exposed to the sun, seedlings began poking their heads up from the old garden area. At first, Hume was unsure of their significance, since the immature leaves of little plantlets make identification difficult. However, he soon discovered that he had found some of Peter O'Reilly's hollyhocks, sprouting from seeds that had been dormant for six decades. Other evidence confirmed the discovery. The plants grew to be 12 feet tall with single blooms, unusual in a day when most modern hollyhocks are far shorter and carry double flowers.

Today, these hollyhocks are themselves aiding the restoration efforts at Point Ellice. They and other historical plants are sold at the house, with the proceeds going toward further research and restoration of the grounds.

grown at Point Ellice, because researchers found written evidence in diaries, letters, or on bills of sale, but no mention was ever made of exactly where in the landscape they were located. Finally, there are those plants never mentioned by the O'Reillys, but that were popular with Victorian gardeners and were likely to have been planted at Point Ellice. Using these classes as a guide, restoration experts are able to piece the landscape back together again.

Providing exact locations for structures in the garden, even when pieces survive, is also a challenge. During a site cleanup, former curator Michael Zarb came across a badly rotted section of plain lumber. He presumed the wood to be a fence post because it seemed to have a hold where a crosspiece would have fit. However, having no time to investigate further, he bagged the find and stored it. Soon thereafter, garden historian Hume started combing the grounds and found a number of half-inch-thick iron rods lying near the post. Little bits of paint, an unearthed latch, and evidence from period photos provided the final clues. The parts were the remains of a fence that ran from the west end of the kitchen garden, around the back of the greenhouse, and ended at the path that cuts south back into the kitchen garden. Hume also surmised that the metal probably came from a local iron company in which Peter owned an interest and from which he had purchased the kitchen and greenhouse stoves as well as the lawn roller.

But why did Peter O'Reilly build the fence? It could neither contain animals nor keep them out, and it ran along a path that, at first glance, does not seem to need a fence. Then Hume looked again at old photographs and noticed that thick foilage

gladiolas or the hedge mentioned above, have been put back into the same location they had occupied at the turn of the nineteenth century. Then there are the plants that historians know were grew where the fence ran. It suddenly came to him that this fence probably had been intended as a support for climbing plants, such as roses. Recalling that Victorians very much liked to control sight lines and views, he guessed that this fence was probably put up as a screen to block the view of the working kitchen garden and the greenhouse from the window of Peter's study.

The Greenhouse Takes Shape

One of the most important archaeological finds relating to the gardens at Point Ellice is the 1977 discovery of the exact location of the greenhouse. Old insurance maps dating from 1903 noted that the structure was roughly south of the house, and the O'Reilly diaries mentioned the purchase and installation of a heating system. But no details were ever given as to the location of the greenhouse nor to the nature of the heating device.

It was pure luck that the greenhouse foundation was discovered, again by a yard-cleaning crew, this time removing ivy overgrowth near the kitchen garden. Having stumbled upon the foundation walls, they called in curator Zarb. Working slowly with just one assistant, Zarb uncovered the basic foundation of the greenhouse, some of the walls, a potbelly stove outside the greenhouse, and a brick kiln inside. Later archaeologists would determine that the dual heating system was connected to a labyrinth of pipes that ran throughout the greenhouse—a costly and complex assemblage demonstrating once again how important the gardens were to the O'Reilly

---

DIG-LESS ARCHAEOLOGY

When we think of archaeology, we usually imagine a hard-bitten Indiana Jones type overseeing students who painstakingly dig and sift through layers of soil. But just as doctors can use magnetic resonance-imaging machines to look inside your body without resorting to a scalpel, archaeologists can now employ devices that use magnetism to survey subsurface structures without a shovel.

The device is actually quite simple. A handheld transmitter produces a magnetic field that, when passed over the ground, induces a secondary, minute magnetic field in subsurface materials. These tiny magnetic fields can be sensed by a receiver. Underground structures such as walls, bricks, or foundations create magnetic fields that are slightly different from those of the earth that surrounds them. By measuring the changes in these magnetic fields, archaeologists can create a map of underground structures. This technology can be used either to help pinpoint dig locations or as a substitute for actual excavation in places where disturbing the surface would be expensive, undesirable, or prohibited by local ordinance or landowners.

In 1994, a company was hired to use this technique to try to find that elusive pathway in the kitchen garden at Point Ellice. Unfortunately, the high-tech search was hampered by a low-tech water pipe that created such a large magnetic field that the results were rendered inconclusive.

---

family and how much money they were willing to spend on them.

Despite the extensive heating system, the greenhouse, called the conservatory by the O'Reillys, was a modest building, standing 7 or 8 feet tall and measuring approximately 14 feet long by 8 feet

The original O'Reilly greenhouse and boiler were accidentally discovered by a garden clean-up crew. Archaeologists later excavated and preserved the remains of the structure, and removed the boiler for safekeeping. The exact means of the greenhouse's demise, and when it occurred, have never been fully understood. Only traces of the foundation remain today, but there is hope that the structure can one day be rebuilt.

kitchen-garden paths. In a nod to modernity, Peter even had the greenhouse wired for electricity so the Point Ellice gardeners could continue working as the days grew short. The lighting, coupled with the extensive heating system, was just some of what Peter O'Reilly spent money on in keeping up the conservatory. The building receipts show that the greenhouse was painted in 1902 by a local handyman. Two years later, the broken glass was replaced and much of the glazing was reputtied. Then, other than a few occasional mentions over the next few years, the greenhouse rather mysteriously disappeared from the records. Perhaps, after Peter's death in 1905, Kathleen was no longer as interested in its use, and simply allowed the structure to sit empty. Or perhaps the declining financial fortunes of the O'Reillys necessitated its closure. Whatever the reason, by World War I the greenhouse seems to have been pretty much abandoned, its slow disintegration and ultimate disappearance from the landscape forming a bleak testament to the ephemeral nature of the garden.

wide. The north wall was solid with no glass, and was sunk 10 inches into the clay soil by the builders, presumably to help hide it from the house. Archaeologists found a number of small metal sheets, which they believe were used to cover broken panes of glass in the walls. The only door, in the east wall, leads onto one of the main

For advice on digging up the past in your own yard, see page 129 in the appendix.

That headlong ivy! Not a leaf will grow
But thinking of a wreath . . .

—ELIZABETH BARRETT BROWNING,
Aurora Leigh

Of all the plants romanticized by the Victorians, ivy was probably the favorite. In fact, to achieve this popularity, ivy had literally to climb its way out of obscurity. It's fair to say that ivy was everywhere in the Victorian age, both inside and out.

There are many kinds of ivy: English ivy, which is native to England and parts of Asia with temperate weather, was used as signs over taverns. This woody evergreen vine whoses berries are poisonous is touted as the most popular house and wall ivy. Other popular varieties are Boston (*Parthenocissus tricuspidata*) and Virginia creeper (*P. quinquefolia*). Ivies can be used as ground cover as well as a way of covering up ruins. It is also said that ivy was sacred to Bacchus and featured prominently in many pagan rituals.

While ivy had been known and grown since classical times, it didn't find terrific favor in the garden until the picturesque movement in the arts came to the fore in the late 1700s. Then its happy habit of climbing over anything left in place for too long, especially ancient ruins (or not so ancient ruins, like the remains of the greenhouse at Point Ellice), made it instantly popular for rendering a feeling of gothic romance in even the newest garden. Ivy be-

came a gardening hit, with the number of varieties rising from a half dozen mostly green types before the dawn of the Victorian age to several hundred, including many variegated ivies, by the time Shirley Hibberd wrote a delightful little tome specifically dedicated to the plant in 1872.

In the O'Reilly garden, ivy was originally used chiefly as an edging material for flower beds and borders. Its natural propensity to

I V Y

spread over the decades means it now appears more widely through the grounds than previously intended. Elsewhere, though, its

uses were much more diverse: everything from the stuff of topiary standards to bedding out specimens. Large pots of ivy, 6 to 12 feet high, were commonly sold in large urban nurseries to provide instant screening for city gardens. Indoors, the plant was everywhere. Ivy was recommended for wreathing picture frames (using a cleverly conceived wedge-shaped pot attached to the back of the frame), trailing around sofas and couches to form shady bowers, over large arches on the dinner table (with pots suitably hidden under the table surface), and was even trained into portable fire screens (presumably used only in the off-season).

Of course the hard-pressed ivy could lend itself to these diversions because it is such a hardy plant. Tolerant of shade, and capable of withstanding the fumes and temperature fluctuations of typical Victorian rooms, ivy was one of the few plants that could stand up to such harsh conditions and still thrive.

So if you're looking to add a little period greenery to your decor, whether inside or out, why not try ivy? Fortunately, many of the frames and other contrivances used to train ivy into special shapes are still made today, and are available through specialty shops and catalogues. All you need are some pots of your favorite variety, a pair of scissors, some ingenuity, and a bit of patience. Given enough time, that "headlong" ivy will form itself into the perfect period garden ornament.

EPILOGUE

- BY -

JOHN ADAMS, REGIONAL MANAGER, BC HERITAGE

Afterglow

With Caroline's death in 1899, followed by Peter's in 1905, the three O'Reilly children became equal inheritors of the Point Ellice estate. Eldest son Frank, returning in 1906 from his engineering practice in Argentina, decided to make Point Ellice his home, along with the two still-single siblings already living there—Jack, the lawyer, and Kathleen, now acting as lady of the house. During the idyllic last years before World War I, the three O'Reillys maintained most of the halcyon traditions their Gilded Age parents had known: Garden parties, social engagements, and frequent foreign travel continued unabated, thanks in large part to the wise investments Peter O'Reilly had made for his children. Indeed, the opening months of that fateful year, 1914, found all three O'Reillys enjoying extended stays in Europe, the two sons for very special reasons—both had found English brides. Jack married Mary Windham in January 1914, and

Frank married Jessie Blakiston in April of that same year.

Returning to Victoria before the outbreak of hostilities, Frank and Jessie took up residence at Point Ellice House. Jack and Mary, still in England at war's onset, decided to remain there, where Jack served first in the Royal Navy, then as a major with the Army Air Service. Kathleen, who was literally trapped in England with the outbreak of fighting, was unable to leave until the war's conclusion. She returned to Victoria in 1918 with Jack and Mary, and all three moved into Point Ellice House with Frank. Frank's wife, Jessie, unhappy with her marriage, had two years previously decamped back to England with their two children, never to return. Jack and Mary later had one son, John, who was born in 1920.

During the decade that followed, Frank and Jack continued to earn money in their respective professions, but the two boys and Kathleen relied heavily on the income from their inheritance to maintain

Clockwise from top left: The original O'Reilly croquet stand containing a variety of mallets, balls, and original hoops; boudoir flower vases; a detail of the roof line; an elegant porcelain teapot from one of Caroline's several tea sets; various glass flower vases; an early sprinkler that shot a stream of water almost 30 feet; a cast-iron teakettle and enamel-lined kitchen pots; an ornamental bracket on the veranda.

the same lifestyle they had known before the war, one that was rapidly becoming more than they could afford. The family's tenuous financial situation in the 1920s was further aggravated by several substantial financial reversals, especially in real estate. As funds became less and less available, Point Ellice House and its grounds began to show a far less manicured appearance than that of Peter and Caroline's day. While the O'Reillys were still able to live more comfortably at Point Ellice House than many families during the subsequent decades (Kathleen, for example, took lavish trips to England and Europe during the late 1920s and 1930s), times were never quite the same again. The last major renovations to the house under Kathleen's guidance took place in 1939 on the eve of World War II. Dilapidated outbuildings were removed, porches were rebuilt, drains were repaired, interior floors were sanded and varnished, gutters were replaced, and exterior painting was done. These repairs, however, were to be the last for several decades. The gardens, already well past their Victorian prime, continued their slow decline.

Nor was the area around Point Ellice to fare any better. In some ways, the bucolic setting around Point Ellice House had been at risk almost from the beginning. Due to its easy access via rapid transit, both by road and water, as early as the 1860s the neighborhood began to fall prey to industrial encroachment, at first from the south, then eventually from all directions. Between about 1860 and the mid-1920s, the only road access to Point Ellice from downtown Victoria was across the Rock Bay Bridge, just south of Point Ellice House. It was here around the shores of Rock Bay that the first industries were established, starting

with the Albion Iron Works and the Victoria Gas Works in the early 1860s. These were later followed by tanneries, sawmills, shingle mills, shipyards, machine shops, match factories, and other plants, until by 1900 the approach to Point Ellice was heavily industrialized.

Still, Pleasant Street and the immediate environs of Point Ellice House remained more or less intact until the 1880s, when the first small sawmill was built along the northern frontage of the house. This site was later expanded and followed by others through the 1920s. Directly west across Selkirk Water from Point Ellice, another fashionable residential neighborhood that had developed in the 1880s and 1890s was affected by the construction of the Canadian Northern Railway's trestle in 1918 and the subsequent development of railyards. Though many early residents would have viewed these new industries as a sign of prosperity (from which many of them, like the O'Reillys, directly benefited as owners or shareholders), fifty years after the O'Reillys had moved into their new house with its lot carved from the virgin forest, the general area beyond the pastoral oasis of Pleasant Street had become a noisy, smoky, smelly, and generally unpleasant place to live.

Descent

As grim and immediate as the industrial encroachment may have been, until the 1930s Point Ellice House was buffered to some extent by the O'Reillys' own property and the houses and gardens of their neighbors. Several factors contributed to the ultimate end of Pleasant Street as a

The neighborhood around Point Ellice today. Only the flower banner and an ornate fence post hint of the gardens to be found within. Although the outlook for the area around Point Ellice seems to be improving, reversing almost a century of decline won't be easy.

fashionable place to live. The O'Reillys forfeited several adjacent lots (across the street and beside their house to the north) to the City of Victoria through tax default in the 1930s. The Drake family's house (next door to Point Ellice House to the south) was demolished in the 1930s. When a tie mill was built on the former Drake property, Frank blamed the City of Victoria for allowing—even en- couraging—the encroachment through its zoning, and in the late 1930s wrote to complain bitterly about the changes taking place. By then, however, the O'Reillys' influence had waned and there were no neighbors left to support their position. The en- tire area was rezoned for heavy industry, and one by one the remaining homes fell to the wreckers, until by the late 1950s, Point Ellice House was the only house left within two blocks. Parking lots, gravel yards, paint factories, ever-expanding sawmills, and the massive Victoria Machinery Depot dominated the area by the 1950s.

The family had at one time hoped to redeem their forfeited property, but the disruption of World War II and declining family circumstances prevented that. Frank died in 1941; Kathleen in 1945; and Jack in 1946. With their passing, the costs and upkeep fell entirely to Jack's widow, Mary Windham O'Reilly, and her son, John. During the war John joined the army, and at war's end, he used his army savings to pay off debts, but the need was too great and the family lost its land per- manently, with little money left to maintain either their house or garden. Gradually, the property fell into decay, but Mary and John continued to live in the house and do what they could. The idea of moving, even if they could have afforded to, was too daunting even to consider, given the genera- tions of family tradition at Point Ellice. Members of the Victoria Historical Society urged them to preserve what they could, but mother and son were resigned to the fact that once they were gone, the inevitable destiny of the house would be as a parking lot for the large sawmill to the north. When Mary died in 1964, this indeed seemed Point Ellice's fate.

Rebirth

Then Inez Whiffen entered the picture. A viva- cious, energetic realtor who was living in Vancou- ver, Inez had met John O'Reilly at a seaside resort on Vancouver Island and romance ensued. When they were married in 1967 they could have sold the property and invested the proceeds in a newer house, but Inez helped John to realize the histori- cal importance of his old family home. Slowly, surely, and with every ounce of energy and all of their savings, they began putting the house and grounds into repair. Their goal, no small feat, was to open Point Ellice as a private museum in 1967, Canada's centennial year. Against the odds, they succeeded. While continuing to live in and restore the house, they opened it to the public that year. But Inez and John soon realized that maintaining and operating a historic house was an extremely expensive proposition. Seeking outside aid, they urged the provincial government to assist them financially or to purchase the house outright from them. In 1974 the government did in fact acquire the house, its contents, and grounds outright for $500,000 Canadian, a figure well below the total value of the combined assets. Inez and John continued to live in the house for another year as resident curators during the transition; they then moved and left operation of Point Ellice House to professional curators employed by the provincial government.

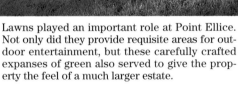

Lawns played an important role at Point Ellice. Not only did they provide requisite areas for outdoor entertainment, but these carefully crafted expanses of green also served to give the property the feel of a much larger estate.

From 1974 to 1987 Michael Zarb brought his investigative abilities to bear on Point Ellice House and its grounds. It was a curator's dream: a treasure trove of O'Reilly family artifacts crammed into closets, attics, drawers, the cellar, and every room in the house—even the carriage shed. He estimated there were ten thousand artifacts in all, but the ongoing cataloguing process suggests the total will likely reach fifteen thousand. The collection's greatest strengths are its breadth, scope, and completeness. In the nineteenth century, the family could afford to buy the best, and did, and their unused or broken items often were kept and stored. Though the family occasionally sold or gave away some objects, their household effects remain mostly intact and represent the most complete collection of Victoriana still in its original setting anywhere in western Canada. Even original wallpapers from the 1860s and 1870s remain hanging in the hallway and master bedroom, with spare rolls still on hand.

Curator Zarb initially devoted his attention to the contents of the house, but soon began to explore and document the gardens. He scoured the beaches in front of the property, crept through the undergrowth and combed the tangled gardens, sometimes digging test holes to find clues about past activities. Professional archaeologists were hired to find out more about key areas, such as the kitchen garden. In 1982 Cyril Hume received the first of several contracts to assist in garden research and planning. His many hours spent documenting the gardens and consulting records in the British Columbia Archives resulted in the plan that ultimately formed the basis for future garden restoration.

In-depth research about the garden and the contents of the house has been possible because the

O'Reilly family wrote copious letters and kept diaries and account books, most of which still exist. This makes Point Ellice House the envy of many historic house museums since so much background information is available. Shopping lists for trips to England, invoices from London stores, shipping manifests for the goods sent to Victoria around Cape Horn, the bill for cartage from the dock to the house, personal letters that describe what objects were in daily use, and inventories made before the O'Reillys' next trip abroad all provide a wealth of detail about the vast collection of artifacts.

Today and the Future

Today, Point Ellice House is an oasis of historical charm in a sea of heavy industry. Log booms, moored in the water below the garden as recently as 1990, are gone now. The sawmills have closed, and their sites are being redeveloped for offices, housing, and light industry. Recycling plants dominate the neighborhood, but through the 1990s boulevard beautification and nonindustrial commercial developments have also changed the appearance of the area. The City of Victoria adopted a new community plan for the district in the mid-1990s, which maintains the heavy industrial zoning, while recommending the long-term development of a park on the old Drake property. Noise, dust, and heavy truck traffic are the main conservation and operational problems for Point Ellice House as a historic site, especially on weekdays.

What does the future hold for Point Ellice House? After many years, the house has been structurally stabilized; now the lengthy process of restoring interior rooms can begin, starting with the dining room. The gardens have not looked better since the early 1900s but the restoration is not yet complete. Overmature elm trees, especially along the southern property line, should be removed to allow more sunlight into the kitchen garden, but they have been left standing because they form a screen that successfully blocks unsightly views and cuts down on noise. Eventually the kitchen garden and other perimeter areas will be restored in keeping with the rest of the grounds. In the meantime, reconstructing the greenhouse on the edge of the kitchen garden is a

The front approach to Point Ellice.

project that would enhance the function and understanding of the gardens and is a priority when funds allow.

If You Go

Point Ellice House is located close to downtown Victoria but is hidden from main roads. Technically its address is 2616 Pleasant Street, but most residents of Victoria won't know where that is if they are asked for directions. The easiest way to get there by car is to drive along Bay Street from downtown and look for the last street on the right hand side, just before the Point Ellice (aka Bay Street) Bridge. A large directional sign points the way. A nicer way to arrive is by harbor ferry from the inner harbor. Ferries have a regular service every half hour during the peak summer season, about every hour at other times.

Point Ellice House is open to the public every day from mid-May to mid-September, 10:00 A.M. to 5:00 P.M., and at Halloween and Christmas for special programs. Group tours may be arranged throughout the year. Afternoon tea in the garden from May to September is a special treat enjoyed by many visitors. Advance reservations are recommended but not always essential.

Information and reservations: (250) 380-6506

Web sites: General information:
    www.heritage.gov.bc.ca

Collections database, virtual tour (house and garden):
    www.collections.ic.gc.ca/peh

APPENDIX

PERIOD PROJECTS, PARTICULARS,
- AND -
PECULIARITIES

Laying Out Your Yard • Tips for Hedges and Border Screens • Period Shrubs for Hedging

Building Gravel Walks and Drives • To Curve or Not to Curve—That Was the Question

Building Your Own Cold Frames • Cold Frames and Hot Beds

Planting a Victorian Window Box • Seasonal Recipes for Victorian Window Gardening

Make Your Own Wardian Case • Roses at Point Ellice • Creating a Victorian Bouquet

Plantspeak, or the Language of Flowers • Hosting a Victorian Garden Tea Party

Playing Croquet the Victorian Way • Espaliered Fruit Trees • Naturalizing Bulbs

Digging Up the Past • Kitchen Garden Recipes

If you are thinking about designing, or redesigning, your own yard, you should begin as Peter O'Reilly most certainly did: Make a simple general plan of your property.

It cannot be too strongly impressed upon the readers mind that most grounds, and all that are nearly level, can be much better arranged on paper, where all parts are under the eye at the same moment, than upon the ground, while planting.

—FRANK SCOTT,
Suburban Home Grounds

This initial plan doesn't have to be fancy: In fact at this stage, it's best just to make large circles to indicate what complements you intend to include where. Often you will find that function drives form. Just like at Point Ellice House, a vegetable garden needs to go in the sunniest spot possible; outdoor living areas need easy access to the house and bright, breezy locations; work areas are often best tucked out of sight nearest where the work needs to be done; siting for front and drive approaches will be imposed by the house architecture.

The danger in all this is that it is very easy to create so many little spaces that you run the risk of making the property look small and uninviting, and that individual spaces themselves become too tiny to be truly functional. At Point Ellice House, Peter avoided this mistake by limiting the number of divisions to four or five, and by making

sure that these individual areas of the landscape were large and spacious, with ample sight lines both through the property to other areas beyond and from one area of the garden to another.

This concept of sight lines was an extremely important consideration in the Victorian era, and one that is generally

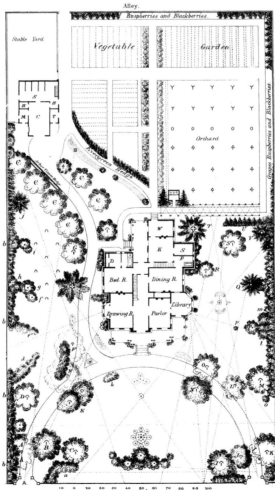

A typical Victorian plan.

overlooked today. If you glance at any landscape plan of the period, like this 1870 plan from Frank Scott's *Suburban Home Grounds*, you will see a number of thin dashed lines radiating out from the house through the various portions of the gardens. These are the sight lines, and they were a major consideration in how the garden was ultimately laid out. Unlike today, where we have the tendency to plan the outside of our properties as if they had no relationship at all to the interior, Victorians like the O'Reillys were very much concerned about how the landscape was seen not only from the street, but also from the house and other areas of the garden.

The house must always be regarded as the chief point of vision in a place and the best views of the grounds should consequently be had from it. The windows of a house are most used for looking at a garden, and the points of interest can there be inspected more leisurely. For these reasons, and because occasional visitors see a garden more from the windows of the house, it is a good plan in laying out a garden to form a series of lines radiating from one, two or three principal windows . . . towards the outside boundary, and to place requisite specimens and groups of plants solely within certain of the triangles thus made . . . never suffering the specimens nearest the house to be so large as to cover the greater space at the broad end of the triangle.

—EDWARD KEMP,
How to Lay Out a Small Garden

Following this advice, at Point Ellice House plantings were laid out to create a number of long vistas that "borrowed" the landscape of the surrounding areas while giving an expansive feel to the spaces within. The views from the dining-room windows that extended through the front gates to what was then fields and pasture, as well as the lovely views across the croquet grounds to the Selkirk Water, the bridge and wooded hills beyond, are good examples of this idea.

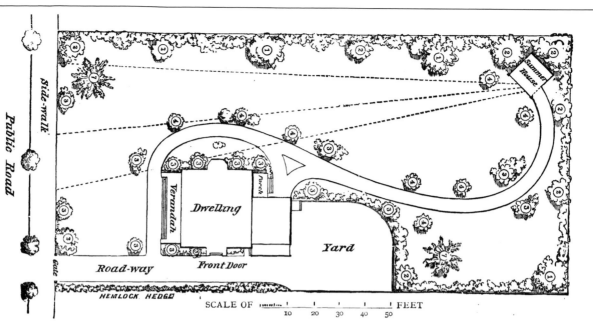

As period guides show, interior views within the garden were also important. The paths, fencing, and hedges were all laid out to provide windows that allowed brief glimpses of the garden areas beyond, without overly exposing the areas within and without. These garden windows created a series of visual vignettes that gave a sense of mystery to the garden—continuing glimpses of what lay beyond that drew you from one area into another and linked the whole garden together.

It's not hard to create this same kind of effect in your own garden—especially if you keep this idea of sight lines in mind right from the start. The first step is to make a scale drawing of your house and garden, either by the old-fashioned method of using a tape measure and graph paper, or by the new, using a computer landscape design program. Either way, the process is the same. Once the outlines of the house, called the footprint, are in

place and the borders and any other main features of the property are charted out, take a walk around the inside of the house and note the views from the windows where you and your family spend the most time, both on the first and upper floors. Draw sight lines from the location of the windows to the views beyond. Note, too, any unpleasant views that should be blocked or modified. Then do the same from the street looking toward the house. While it's important to make sure you have some privacy for the house and garden, unless it's absolutely necessary, try not to create a walled effect with fencing or plantings that completely block the view of the house and grounds from the road. The Victorian ideal was to be able to catch tantalizing glimpses of the house and its lovely garden from the street, while still maintaining a distinct border between the public and private areas of the property. That should be your goal as well.

Within the garden itself, try to achieve

this same effect by creating framed views. Mark down on your plan the dividing elements that separate the various areas of the garden into rooms, and make sure that there are visual connections between the areas that allow for the vistas from one area to another. Pathways, gates, arbors, and stretches of lawn framed by shrubs are great for this. A Victorian precept that the O'Reillys followed closely was to allow for at least one or two interior sight lines that revealed the greatest possible distance across the property. At Point Ellice House, there are several: a long view across the front from the entrance gates through the rose arch to the cutting garden beyond; a long view from the front fence across the cutting garden and croquet lawn; and finally, the most spectacular of all, the view across the croquet lawn to the flower beds, woods, and the Selkirk Water beyond. While each area is defined and distinct, these window views link the separate pieces of the garden into a cohesive whole.

While hedges were generally not part of the ornamental landscape during the Victorian period, they were very much the workhorse of more practical areas, so it's important to know how to grow them well. This might seem a rather straightforward affair, but the successful designing, planting, and maintaining of hedges and border screens can be surprisingly tricky. Keeping these tips in mind will help.

• Hedges, a fairly formal linear planting of a single species, essentially form a living, breathing garden fence. As such, they need to start, and terminate, at points that complete the containment of a particular area, just as a fence would. Border screens, which are more naturalistic, non-linear groupings of different plants, can be used much more informally and can often form islands to block or frame a particular view.

• With both hedges and border screens, be sure to consider the ultimate height of the planting required, and its scale relative to the overall landscape. First ask yourself what you are trying to screen out. Is there a view you want to hide, or do you just need something low to delineate a particular space? Do you need a plant that will only grow 10 feet high and stop, or do you need something higher? Remember that views depend greatly on perspective, and you can often use a much shorter planting by positioning the screen closer to your vantage point, as shown below. Consider too the ground space you have available to donate to the planting. Many plants grow as wide as they are tall, and benighted homeowners who unsuspectingly plant such spreading varieties are left with a never-ending battle trying to contain them in their misallotted space. The trick is to find shrubs that grow only in the direction you want them to. If ground space is at a premium, look for narrow, upright varieties; they are often, though not always, labeled with the Latin *columnaris* (columnar), and are ideal for situations where height is required with little room for width.

• Are your privacy concerns seasonal? For instance, is the area in question only used during the summer? If so, you may want to plant a deciduous border. Deciduous plants have the advantage of having a far greater selection of interesting fruit, flower, and foliage possibilities than their evergreen cousins. Deciduous hedges are generally far less expensive to plant as well. The trade-off is, of course, that privacy is only provided for half of the year. There are plants appropriate for every condition, and an equal number that are not. Consulting a good guide, or an experienced garden professional, will save you from making costly and laborious mistakes.

• It's imperative to keep in mind growing conditions along the entire line of the proposed planting. This is especially true of hedges, which depend on uniformity for their success. Unlike fencing, which is obviously indifferent to growing conditions, natural barriers require uniform light, fertility, and water conditions along the full line to achieve the best effect.

If you have chosen a hedge that needs shearing to keep its form, be sure to pay attention to the way you trim it. Many a good hedge is ruined by not following this simple rule: To remain full, hedges should be trimmed to be wider on the bottom than on the top. To some extent, the reason people fail to do this is that they are simply following the natural lines of the shrub. Many hedging materials such as box or privet are naturally wider at the top or in the middle than they are on the bottom. Left to themselves the plants have a tendency to shade out their own lower growth as they age. While this matters to the plant not a whit, it can defeat the entire purpose of the line for the hedge owner when large unsightly gaps appear. The problem is compounded by many garden-

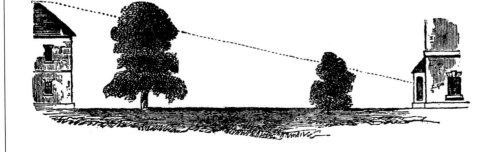

ers when they prune: Following the natural lines of the shrub creates even denser growth that further shades out the lower leaves. Instead, do as the Victorians did—"batter" your hedge—shearing it so that the base is wider than the top, allowing light to fall equally on all branches. This will ensure thick, uniform coverage over the entire surface of the plant.

And while on the subject of pruning: If you have inherited an old deciduous hedge or screen planting that is barren at the bottom, you can often rejuvenate the planting by cutting the hedge down in the fall to 6 inches or so above the ground. While this may sound rather drastic, many plants respond very well to such treatment, and in any case it's the only way to force a plant to re-leaf its lower reaches. An established planting such as privet, lilac, or spirea will often rebound to its former height in a few short years much thicker for its radical haircut. One important note, however: This method only works for certain deciduous plantings. Evergreens must be slowly reduced over a period of years a few inches at a time, once a season just after the first flush of new growth. More rapid reductions will often result in the death of the plant.

PERIOD SHRUBS FOR HEDGING

The following were all introduced before 1900.

EVERGREEN SHRUBS/TREES
Buxus microphylla and varieties
Chamaecyparis pisifera
Cupressus sempervirens
Euonymus fortunei radicans
E. fortunei 'Vegetus'
E. japonicus
Ilex aquifolium
I. cornuta
I. crenata and varieties
I. glabra 'Compacta'
Juniperus chinensis and varieties
J. scopulorum and varieties
J. virginiana and varieties
Ligustrum japonicum
L. lucidum
Mahonia aquifolium
Osmanthus heterophyllus
Picea abies
P. glauca
P. glauca 'Conica'
P. omorika
P. orientalis
P. pugens and varieties
Pinus resinosa
P. strobus
Pittosporum tobira
Taxus baccata
T. baccata 'Erecta'
T. baccata 'Repandens'
T. canadensis 'Stricta'
T. cuspidata

T. cuspidata 'Nana'
T. media 'Kelseyi'
T. media 'Sentinalis'
T. media 'Stoveken'
Thuja occidentalis
T. occidentalis 'Douglasii Pyramidalis'
T. occidentalis 'Hetz Junior'
T. occidentalis 'Hetz Midget'
T. occidentalis 'Little Champion'
T. occidentalis 'Pumila'
T. occidentalis 'Wareana'
T. orientalis and varieties
Tsuga canadensis
T. caroliniana
Viburnum prunifolium
V. tinus

PLANTS WITH DENSE FOLIAGE
Acanthopanax sieboldianus
Acer ginnala
Baccharis halimifolia
Berberis koreana
B. thunbergii
B. thunbergii 'Erecta'
B. thunbergii 'Minor'
Betula populifolia
Carpinus betulus
Chaenomeles speciosa
Cornus mas
C. racemosa

Crataegus crus-galli
C. phaenopyrum
Euonymus alatus 'Compactus'
Fagus grandifolia
F. sylvatica 'Fastigiata'
Ilex vomitoria
Ligustrum amurense
L. obtusifolium regelianum
L. ovalifolium
Lonicera fragrantissima
L. maackii
L. maackii podocarpa
L. nitida
L. tatarica
Philadelphus lemoinei 'Avalanche'
P. lemoinei 'Erectus'
Prinsepia sinensis
Pyracantha coccinea 'Lalandei'
Rhamnus frangula
R. frangula 'Columnaris'
Ribes alpinum
Rosa multiflora
R. rugosa
Spiraea vanhouttei
Stephanandra incisa 'Crispa'
Syringa josikaea
S. persica
S. villosa
Ulmus pumila
Viburnum lantana
V. lentago

V. opulus 'Compactum'
V. opulus 'Nanum'
V. trilobum 'Compactum'

LOW-GROWING SHRUBS
Cotoneaster lucida
Hypericum varieties

SHRUBS WITH THORNS
Hippophae rhamnoides
Poncirus trifoliata
Rosa virginiana

FLOWERING SHRUBS
Hydrangea arborescens 'Grandiflora'
H. macrophylla
Philadelphus coronarius
Spiraea arguta
S. prunifolia
S. thunbergii
Syringa chinensis
S. persica
S. vulgaris
Tamarix parviflora
T. pentandra

COLORED FRUITS
Aronia arbutifolia
Cornus alba
Euonymus alatus
Viburnum dentatum

BUILDING GRAVEL WALKS AND DRIVES

The Victorians, true to form, never did anything halfway, and that included gravel walks and drives. Unlike today, where the average contractor or homeowner simply makes an excavation of several inches, pours in some gravel, and calls it a day, Victorian gravel walks were built according to strict specifications that hadn't changed much since Roman times. Although the process involves considerably more initial work, it's well worth the time and effort. The result is a hard, durable surface that keeps dry even in the wettest weather, doesn't rut or splay, resists weeds and will last far longer than modern imitations. To quote Kemp in *How to Lay Out a Small Garden*, from whom these specifications are adapted:

> *Very much of the pleasure of a garden will depend on the manner in which its walks are formed. A walk that becomes muddy or slimy in wet weather or after frosts, or allows the water to lodge upon it during and after rains, or has a surface of course and harsh or loose materials, will do much towards deterring persons from using their gardens so constantly, or at least will rob them of a good deal of enjoyment.*

Step One: Excavation

The key to obtaining a good gravel walk is to ensure that the uppermost sections of pathway stay dry in all weather. This is achieved by proper excavation of the ground beneath the gravel. Guides of the day recommend digging out the area in an inverted crescent shape, 9 inches deep in the center, and 16 to 18 inches deep on the sides. As the ground beneath the gravel is considerably less porous than the gravel itself, this excavation has the effect of troughing any excess water off to the sides. As regards width, 4 to 6 feet was considered standard for small, curving garden pathways, 6 to 8 feet for straight walks, and 10 to 14 feet for drives. While this process requires nothing more than several shovels, a heavy-duty wheelbarrow, and a couple of strong backs, those undertaking extensive areas may wish to rent a Bobcat or other small excavator to help with the digging and moving of gravel, a convenience unknown to the Victorians, but one that they surely would have welcomed.

One other note to the modern gardener: The walk widths given above may seem somewhat excessive, but they were originally mandated by the extremely wide and flowing dress fashions of the day. In many cases, 6 feet was just wide enough for a lady and gentleman to walk abreast, which still remains a primary criterion for good walks today. The architecture of the period, with its broad and welcoming porches and entrances, also demanded rel-

An early picture of Peter O'Reilly standing in the front doorway of Point Ellice House, about 1880. The crisp, elegant gravel drive left no doubt in the minds of first-time visitors to Point Ellice that they were about to meet people of distinction.

atively wide walks to maintain a relative sense of scale. While you may wish to narrow the path dimensions slightly in your garden, especially on smaller sites, keep in mind that any principal walkways designed for daily traffic should not be narrower than 5 feet.

Conversely, driveway widths were considerably narrower in the Victorian era. Since parking cars was obviously not an issue, drives only needed to be wide enough to allow for easy dismounting from a horse or carriage—rarely a concern today. In general, modern driveways should be wide enough to accommodate fully opened car doors, at a minimum 12 feet. A drive designed to allow two cars to pass needs to be at least 18 feet wide. If you're in doubt about the space you'll need, drive a car or two onto the proposed space and try out different configurations. You can also consult a good guide like the *Reader's Digest Book of Home Landscaping*, which lists parking and turnaround distances for most types of drives.

Step Two: Filling the Lowest Layer

The next step is to fill your excavation with stone, being careful not to fill the entire depth with the same fine gravel intended for the surface. The result will be a mushy upper level that will never firm up sufficiently to walk upon. The bottom of the excavation, and especially the deeper side portions intended as drainage areas, should be filled with old broken bricks, small rocks and stones, clinkers, or whatever other type of stone is available to within 6 inches of the surface. It was broken brick pieces like these, in fact, that initially lead archaeologists excavating at Point Ellice to theorize that the gravel walks had at one time been made of brick,

an idea pretty much since discarded. If sufficient garden debris is not available, order the largest size crushed stone you can find at your local gravel yard.

Step Three: Filling the Upper Layers

On top of this very rough material, pour in $1/2$ to 1 inch pieces of crushed stone to within 2 or 3 inches of the top. Water the mix thoroughly with a hose at full pressure and then rake. After the path is watered and graded, roll with a garden roller (or use a manual or mechanical tamper, the latter available at most home rental stores). At this stage, the upper layers should be well compacted and completely solid underfoot.

Step Four: The Final Layers

The top layer of the path or drive should be comprised of either very finely crushed, screened gravel like that used at Point Ellice, which often has some clay content to help bind the surface or, for a more rustic look, fine naturally rounded gravel. This material is often called in the trade $1/4$-inch river-washed pea stone. There was considerable debate in the style books of the time as to what was the best color of gravel for landscaping purposes. Whitish gray was generally considered least suitable, due to the cold harshness of its tone, while tannish/reddish gravel was generally the preferred color. While the exact gravel colors available to you will depend on your locality, novices are generally surprised at the number of choices available, so that it pays to make a trip to the gravel yard before you decide. After you have made your selection, spread the gravel over the

crushed stone to the depth of 2 or 3 inches, so that there is a slight rise or crown at the center of the walkway, 1 inch of rise for each 3 feet of walkway width. Once the gravel has been spread, water, roll, rake, and roll again until the surface is hard and firm.

Step Five: Don't Forget the Edgings

As already noted, all good Victorian walkways had edgings. Without them, gravel will splay into the adjoining areas causing a very messy appearance. To quote Mr. Kemp again:

What very much affects the character of walks is the way in which their edgings are laid. These should be quite smooth . . . kept at a uniform distance throughout, and for some part of their width at least, precisely on the same level at both sides . . . though not more than half an inch above the level of the walk. Walks that are not carefully formed in accordance with these conditions will appear more or less slovenly, deficient in the expression of art, and indicative of an unrefined taste.

Step Six: Feeding and Care

And after you've finished, don't neglect the maintenance. Gravel walks should be raked and rolled several times a year to redistribute any errant stones. And even well-made gravel walks and drives sprout the occasional weed, especially in areas of light traffic. Any encroachers can be removed manually. Or you may wish occasionally to use a herbicide like Roundup, or for organic gardeners, hot water and rock salt to control more serious outbreaks. Every three or four years, a new topdressing of gravel will keep your drive or walk looking like new.

TO CURVE OR NOT TO CURVE—
THAT WAS THE QUESTION

Perhaps no other design topic provoked such intense debate in period landscape manuals than the correct way to lay out walks and drives. Practically every book published on the subject dealt with the problem, though perhaps none so amusingly as this passage from Peter Henderson's *Gardening for Pleasure*, 1893. Unfortunately, the problems of overly errant walks and constricting drives still vex garden design today as your almost sure recognition of the issues below will shortly prove. Who among us hasn't encountered these same situations in our gardens more than a hundred years later?

It is no unusual thing to see the owner of a neat cottage make himself perfectly ridiculous by the way in which he lays out the walk from the street to his front door. There is a prevailing opinion that such walks should be curved ones, and gentlemen, often otherwise shrewd and intelligent, place themselves without question in the hands of some self-styled "garden architect," and thus manage to make themselves the laughing stock of a neighborhood.

There was a well marked instance of this in a garden occupying a block in almost the center of Jersey City, where a man pretending to have a full knowledge of the subject, induced the proprietor to have a walk running about one hundred yards from the street to the house, made so curved that its length was nearly twice the distance. It was hard on the butcher's and grocer's boys, and it was said that even book-peddlers, sewing-machine agents, and lightning-rod men looked ruefully at it and left him in peace.

Some old authority on this subject says that there "never should be any deviation from a straight line unless from some real or apparent cause." So if curved lines are insisted on, a tree, rock, or building must be placed at the bend as a reason for going around such obstacles. It will be evident to any one who reflects upon the matter, that a curved walk running a distance of a hundred yards or so, from the street to the house, across an unplanted lawn, is utterly absurd. All short foot-walks from the street to the house should be straight, entering from the street at as near right angles as possible, and leading direct to the front door. There should be no necessity for a carriage road to the front entrance of a house, unless it is distant at least 100 feet from the street, and then a drive is best made by having an entrance at each side of the lot. . . .

The width of the roads or walks must be governed by the extent of the grounds. For carriage-way the width should be no less than ten feet, and for foot-walks, five-feet. Nothing is more annoying than to have a shower-bath in early morning from the dew from an overhanging branch in your narrow walk. We often see gardens of considerable pretensions where the walks are not more than three feet wide, where it is utterly impossible for two persons to walk abreast without getting their dresses torn or faces scratched by overhanging branches. Besides, it argues a narrowness in the owner, particularly if the grounds are at all extensive, and looks as if he were determined to cultivate every foot of land. Of course, it is another matter when the garden plot is limited to the width of a city lot (20 or 25 feet); then such economy of space is perfectly excusable.

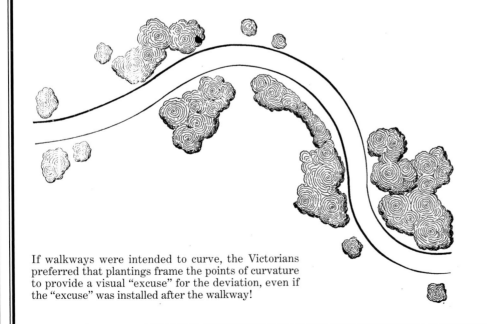

If walkways were intended to curve, the Victorians preferred that plantings frame the points of curvature to provide a visual "excuse" for the deviation, even if the "excuse" was installed after the walkway!

BUILDING YOUR OWN COLD FRAMES

Building a cold frame is an easy, do-it-yourself project, and one that can be accomplished in a few hours some snowy weekend. For this simple model you'll need an 8 x 4-foot sheet of exterior plywood, two pressure-treated 8-foot 1 x 2s (or similar scrap lumber to make stakes), a box of 1½-inch screws, some exterior paint or stain, two door hinges, and finally an old storm window, which can generally be found for the taking in the basement of any old house owner in your acquaintance. (If all else fails, a heavy duty sheet of Plexiglas from the hardware store will work just fine.) Just make sure the window is in good condition before you begin repairing any broken or loose panes.

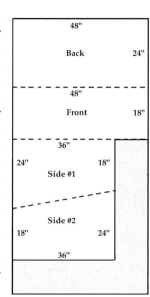

1. Mark out the dimensions right on the sheet of plywood, and draw the lines for cutting. For the purposes of this example, we'll use a 3 x 4-foot storm window, but you can use any size window you have on hand; you'll just need to alter the 48-inch and 36-inch measurements to match the dimensions of your window.

2. Cut out the pieces from the plywood sheet using an electric saw, or have the lumber yard cut out the pieces for you. Cut the 1 x 2s into four pieces: two, 30 inches long, and two, 24 inches long; cut the ends to make four pointed stakes. Attach the two 30-inch stakes to each end of the back of the frame using three screws on each stake. (An electric screw driver is very helpful here.) Use the other two stakes on the front. The pointed end of the stakes should protrude beyond the bottom of the plywood pieces, as shown in the diagram at left.

3. Fasten the sides of the frame to the front and back by screwing them into the sides of the stakes already mounted on the front and back. The body of the cold frame is now complete.

4. Paint the entire assemblage whatever color you choose. Use at least two coats of paint, making sure to cover all surfaces thoroughly.

5. Place the frame in its intended location, and carefully drive the four stakes into the ground with a hammer. In colder climates, you may wish to bury the frame 6 inches or so into the ground for increased insulation.

6. Mount the window to the back side of the frame using the door hinges. To build a double-windowed cold frame similar to the one shown here, simply build two individual frames and place them side by side. A piece of plywood mounted across the front will give the illusion of a single unit.

Kathleen, a friend, and four young girls examining plants growing in cold frames, with a water barrel to the left. When Kathleen was very young she, too, was fascinated with gardening. All of the O'Reilly children had their own garden space, where they tended their plants, experimented with new varieties, and saved their own seeds.

COLD FRAMES AND HOT BEDS

I drove into town with Father and Mother. Went to music lesson....Mother and I potted plants all the afternoon and put them in the new hot bed. Father blew up stumps successfully in new lot.

Here's an annual dilemma that hasn't changed for centuries: You have started your own seeds like Kathleen and Caroline O'Reilly, and they are now several inches high. The plants obviously need more room than you have indoors, and they can't go directly outside. Like fair-skinned blondes in the early spring, seedlings sunburn easily, and need time to get adjusted to the higher light levels and temperature swings found outdoors. If your plant numbers are small, once the weather has warmed up with nights in the 50s, you can set your seedlings in a protected spot out of the direct sun in bright light for a week or two before transplanting them into the garden. But if your quantities are larger, or if you plan to start seeds again next year, you should consider building a cold frame. These delightful devices used to be found in almost every garden, and were once a prominent feature in the Point Ellice kitchen garden, located just to the south of the laurel hedge.

At their simplest, cold frames are just wooden or plastic boxes with a glass top that can be raised. They are called "cold" frames because, unlike a greenhouse or conservatory, they are not actively heated, but rely on the passive heat of the sun.

Cold frames are one of the most useful of all garden structures, and can be used for many purposes such as a growing bed for early spring and fall vegetables, as a place to start seeds or force bulbs, even as extra greenhouse space. When it comes to growing annuals, cold frames are the ideal place to "harden off" (acclimatize) your seedlings to the great outdoors. Snuggled inside the cold frames, the plants are protected from the burning effects of the harsh spring sunlight and temperature swings. The cold frame is a very simple structure to build. An excellent temporary frame can even be made from bales of hay with a sheet of Plexiglas laid on top. You can also purchase a variety of ready-made cold frames directly from a number of suppliers. Once you start using a cold frame, you'll never want to be without one again.

Depending on the type and size of your frame, its inside temperature will generally be about 10-15 degrees warmer than the outside air at night, so you can start using your frames as soon as the night-time temperatures stay in the middle 30s. In many areas of North America, that is most of the winter, in which case cold frames can be used continuously. Altering the construction technique will also help extend the season. While simple frames can be set at ground level, considerably more insulation value is gained by burying the frame slightly so that the interior floor is 8 inches or so below ground level. You can even use a heating cable (like the ones used for starting seeds) to augment the temperature. This idea is not new. Before the advent of electricity, gardeners like the O'Reillys used to set the frames very deeply and cover the inside with 6 inches of fresh manure. The heat given off from the decomposition would keep the inside of such frames at a comfortable 60 degrees for a month or so, converting a cold frame into what was called a hot bed. For those without a greenhouse, winterizing your cold frame with a heat source can provide an almost year-round garden experience, even in the harshest of climates.

Just remember that during the day, particularly in the warm early spring days when the temperatures can soar into the 70s, the cold frame can become a dangerous heat trap that can roast your young plants. Be sure to lift the cover of the frame slightly during the day, to allow the trapped heat to escape, remembering of course to lower it again at night. Automatic openers and closers are now sold for just this purpose. And don't forget to look under the lids at least once a day. Your charges will probably need daily watering.

Seedlings should be left in the cold frame for at least two weeks, and sometimes longer, depending on how big they were when they went in. As the weather warms, you should raise the glass a bit more each day, until the plants have had a chance to become fully acclimated to the sun. They are then ready to be planted in the garden.

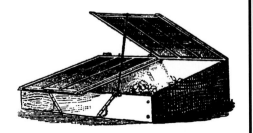

PLANTING A VICTORIAN WINDOW BOX

While you may not have the time or resources to build a complete indoor window garden, you can easily create a window box that will enhance any view.

There are many kinds of window boxes appropriate for period planting. They range from ornate terra-cotta containers to simple wooden boxes painted to match the house. Ideally the size of the box should be approximately the same width as the window.

1. Choose a container with proper drainage holes at its base. If it is wooden, make sure it is painted inside and lined to prevent rotting, or made from some rot-resistant material. For those interested in changing window box displays seasonally, consider using cheap plastic liners that can be easily and quickly lifted out and replaced with new plantings.

2. Cover the bottom of the container with gravel or some other drainage material, such as irregularly shaped stones or pieces of broken pottery. This will allow excess water to drain

out while preventing the holes from becoming clogged with soil.

3. Fill the box within 2 inches of the top, unless you're planting spring bulbs, in which case you'll want only an inch or two of soil over the drainage material. Be sure to use a soil-less potting mix, which is much lighter than normal dirt, retains water better, and is less likely to blow away when dry. You can also mix in water-retaining crystals, available at any garden supply store, to help keep the soil moist.

4. In choosing plants for your box, look for dwarf cultivars and other species that won't grow too big and overwhelm the window. Also, don't neglect plants with interesting foliage. Plants with different-colored leaves like gray act as a foil for brightly colored annuals, toning down their impact and blending them together. Finally, be sure to pay attention to eventual growing heights, placing the taller specimens at the rear and shorter or trailing plants at the front.

5. When planting, make sure your plants are set to the same depth that they were in their original containers.

For bulbs, simply spread them evenly throughout the box and cover with soil to within 2 inches of the top. In both cases, it's best to top off the box with a mulch like shredded bark or buckwheat hulls to slow evaporation. Water the box daily, being careful not to damage the plants with too strong a jet. Feed once a week with a water-soluble fertilizer for extra lush flowers and foliage.

SEASONAL RECIPES FOR
VICTORIAN WINDOW GARDENING

The right combination of flowers in your window boxes will greatly embellish the outside of your abode. John R. Mollison in *The New Practical Window Gardener*, 1877, recommended that window boxes be planted with a wide variety of plants and flowers, changed seasonally. Here's his list of plant groupings for year-round Victorian beauty. Potential window box gardeners take note: Some of Mollison's color combinations may seem a bit bold for modern taste. More muted effects can easily be achieved by substituting plants with a more subtle palette.

Spring Groupings

PRIMARY FLOWERS: Dwarf tulips
ENCOMPASSING FLOWERS: Yellow, white, and blue crocuses, snowdrops

PRIMARY FLOWERS: Late tulips, hyacinths, crocuses, single and double primroses, polyanthus (*Polianthes* sp.)
ENCOMPASSING FLOWERS: Pansies

Early Summer Groupings

PRIMARY FLOWERS: Dwarf wallflowers (*Ersymum* sp.), stocks, and lilies of the valley
ENCOMPASSING FLOWERS: Red and white dwarf daisies, blue pansies

Summer Groupings

PRIMARY FLOWERS: Variegated and scarlet geraniums, brown and yellow slipper flower (*Calceolaria* sp.)
ENCOMPASSING FLOWERS: Blue and white violas, pansies and echevarias, sweet peas at each end to train up along the wall

PRIMARY FLOWERS: Geraniums mixed with little patches of annuals, such as candytuft, nemophilia, clarkias and mignonettes

ENCOMPASSING FLOWERS: Blue lobelias, echevarias, and sedums, canary creeper (*Tropaeolum peregrinum*), nasturtium, and sweet peas

Fall Grouping

PRIMARY FLOWERS: Dwarf asters, chrysanthemums
ENCOMPASSING FLOWERS: Echevarias, blue and yellow violas

Winter Grouping

Ivy mixed with berried twigs of holly, laurel, or other evergreens.

Popular Period Plants for the Winter Window Garden

Nothing is more pleasant in the dead of winter than to come upon a window filled with flowers and scent. Here are some favorite Victorian selections for the inside winter garden, along with some of their attributes.

Azaleas—While sensitive to over- and underwatering, they can be pruned into any shape and come in a wide color range.
Camellias—Most varieties are easy to grow and come in a wide range of colors.
Daphnes—Profusely scented flowers bloom from December to March.
Fuchsias—As either uprights or pruned as standards, fuchsias make colorful indoor specimens.
Geraniums—Both scented and standard varieties make excellent, easy-to-grow houseplants.
Citrus trees—Orange, lemons, and limes were popular parlor plants, valued both for their fruit and highly scented flowers in midwinter.
Roses—China rose (*Rosa chinesesis semperflorens*), crimson in color, was the common rose for window gardening. Called the poor man's friend, the china rose is extremely hardy. The tea rose (*R. odorata*) was introduced in 1812, and its many descendants run the gamut of colors but require more attention than the china rose.
Verbenas—Richly flowering, these plants need little care and were introduced by the dozens during the Victorian period.

Wardian cases (*aka* terrariums) can add an artistic touch to any room. And they are easier to make than you might think, if you follow these simple instructions.

Find the Right Container

Be creative: Antique fruit jars, decanters, wine bottles, and cider jugs are all possibilities. Open globes, old brandy snifters, discarded fishbowls, or aquariums are also commonly used. Two important considerations: The container must be watertight; and it should, by preference, have a lid, cover, or some means such as a cork to close the container and retain humidity.

Choose the Proper Location

Choose a place with diffused, not direct sunlight. Direct sunlight can be magnified through the glass sides of the terrarium. You should also keep the container away from heaters or vents that might cause it to overheat.

Select Appropriate Plants

All the plants in the case need to be compatible. Consult a good guide to make sure they all prefer the same levels of humidity, moisture, and light. Try to choose a selection of tall, medium, and short plants, using one dominant tall plant as the focal point. If the container has tinted glass, pick shade-loving plants with bold leaves that can easily be seen and enjoyed through the glass. Also, if your container has a small aperture, be sure the plants you select can fit through the opening!

Planting Tips

1. Sterilize the container by running it through a dishwasher or cleaning it well with hot, soapy water with a touch of bleach, and rinse thoroughly. Allow it to air dry. The soil in the container should reach no more than one-fourth of the overall height. For instance, a 12-inch container should have a 3-inch soil layer, consisting of $2/3$ inch of drainage material, such as crushed rock or pebbles on the bottom, with a thin layer of charcoal

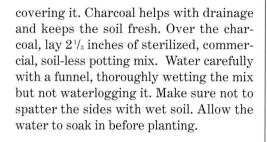

covering it. Charcoal helps with drainage and keeps the soil fresh. Over the charcoal, lay $2\frac{1}{3}$ inches of sterilized, commercial, soil-less potting mix. Water carefully with a funnel, thoroughly wetting the mix but not waterlogging it. Make sure not to spatter the sides with wet soil. Allow the water to soak in before planting.

2. Carefully place your plants, positioning those that will grow the tallest in the rear for one-sided containers, or in the center for those meant to be seen from all sides. For small-mouthed bottles or cases, there are special terrarium tools to assist in placing and planting. (These are available at specialty nurseries, or you can craft your own using clothes hangers and old tableware.)

3. After planting, water *sparingly* with a mister or a turkey baster. Terrariums are remarkably self-sufficient when it comes to water. Often weeks or months will pass before plants in a tightly sealed container will require additional moisture. In large-mouthed containers, you'll know it's time to water when you stick your finger in and find dry soil an inch down. Small-necked containers are trickier to judge, but if the soil appears dry, or moisture no longer beads on the top of the glass, water lightly.

ROSES AT POINT ELLICE

One of the most spectacular aspects of the Point Ellice House garden is the abundance of period roses. Scattered throughout the landscape, whether growing on fences, covering arbors, providing backdrops to the flower borders, or scenting the air beneath a window, roses help to bridge the world of flowers, and shrubs. Pretty much self-tending and subject to very few of the problems that infest their modern cousins, old roses are an ideal way to invoke the romance of the Victorian garden without the labor normally associated with large floral displays.

The box on the following page contains some of the roses known to have been grown at Point Ellice, many of which are still found there today. Fortunately for the old garden aficionado, the tremendous surge of interest in old roses means that many of these varieties are once again available from specialty rose suppliers around the country.

ROSE	TYPE	YEAR OF INTRO-DUCTION	DESCRIPTION
'Archduc Charles'	China	1840	lovely pink, sometimes a very pale blush shade, with cherry-rose edges
'Baroness Rothchild'	Hybrid Perpetual	1868	compact and graceful in habit, with large powder-puff flowers of deep pink, full quartered, and fragrant
'Boule de Neige'	Bourbon	1867	white buds tipped with red open globularly and then reflex nearly to a ball shape
'Captain Christy'	Unknown	1873	much-sought-after buds
'Catherine Mermet'	Tea	1869	exquisitely spiraled, upright flowers of soft, warm pink, tinted peach

ROSE	TYPE	YEAR OF INTRO-DUCTION	DESCRIPTION
'Cabbage Rose'	Centifolia	Ancient	full globular soft pink rose
'Comtesse de Barbabante'	Tea	1858	blush, shaded with rose
'Duchesse de Brabant'	Tea	1857	globose flowers of warm pink
'General Jacqui-menot'	Hybrid Perpetual	1853	pepper-rose scented flowers of deep, plush crimson, with crimson-pink reverses, which turn to bluish-purple
'Gloire de Dijon'	Tea Noisettes	1853	exquisite in color, form, and fragrance; abundant flowers
'Her Majesty'	Hybrid Perpetual	1885	a lilac and lavender-pink bicolor whose large flowers take days to develop
'Hermosa'	China	1840	light blush pink; small, shapely flowers
'Honourine de Brabant'	Bourbon	1840	blooms with stripes and pencilings of violet and mauve over pale pink
'Jean Liabaud'	Unknown	1875	fiery crimson, center rich velvety crimson, flowers large
'La France'	Climbing Hybrid-tea	1867	silvery rose with pale lilac shading, most abundant, highly fragrant
'Louise Odier'	Bourbon	1851	china-pink flowers of formal perfection, domed, quartered, and delicate
'Madam Isaac Pereire'	Bourbon	1881	large, intensely colored claret pink, amaranth, and magenta flowers of surpassing fragrance

'Reverend H. Dombrain'

'Princess Louise Victoria'

ROSE	TYPE	YEAR OF INTRO- DUCTION	DESCRIPTION
'Madam Pierre Oger'	Bourbon	1878	very cupped, smallish flowers of ivory, usually distinctly edged cerise pink, double blooming
'Magna Carta'	Hybrid Perpetual	1876	bright pink, suffused with carmine, very large, full of good form, habit erect, growth vigorous, magnificent foliage
'Marie Van Houtte'	Tea	1871	light yellow, edged with pink, fine exhibition variety, particularly in moist weather
'Meteor'	Bourbon	Unknown	rich deep rose, large petals, shapely flowers, in small clusters
'Mme Honore Defrense'	Unknown	1886	sparkling yellow flowers large, full, very well formed, beautiful dark yellow with coppery reflections
'Mme. Caroline Testout'	Hybrid Tea	1890	bright satiny rose edged with soft carmine pink
'Mme. Falcot'	Tea	1858	deep rich orange-yellow, petals large, flowers not full rich dark foliage
'Mme. Scipion Cochet'	Unknown	1871	purplish pink bordered delicate light pink, flower full, cupped, center petals ruffled
'Mrs. John Laing'	Hybrid Perpetual	1887	silvery lilac pink, superbly fragrant
'Niphetos'	Tea	1843	pure white rose, pale green foliage
'Paul Neyron'	Hybrid Perpetual	1869	bright claret pink, blued to a unique shade tending toward carmine at times
'Perle des Jardins'	Climbing Tea	1890	soft lemon yellow blossoms, with a strong fruity tea fragrance
'Prince Camille de Rohan'	Hybrid Perpetual	1861	medium-size or large, full flower; maroon, crimson, very dark, velvety, nuanced blood red.

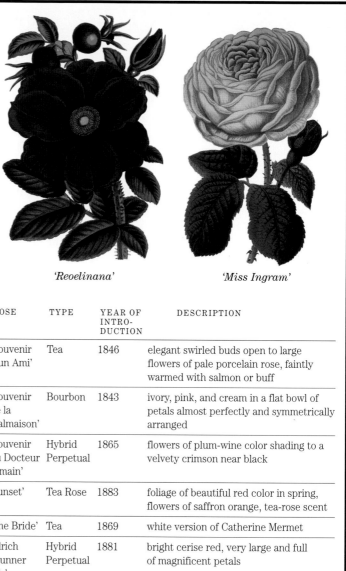

'Reoelinana' 'Miss Ingram'

ROSE	TYPE	YEAR OF INTRO- DUCTION	DESCRIPTION
'Souvenir d'un Ami'	Tea	1846	elegant swirled buds open to large flowers of pale porcelain rose, faintly warmed with salmon or buff
'Souvenir de la Malmaison'	Bourbon	1843	ivory, pink, and cream in a flat bowl of petals almost perfectly and symmetrically arranged
'Souvenir du Docteur Jamain'	Hybrid Perpetual	1865	flowers of plum-wine color shading to a velvety crimson near black
'Sunset'	Tea Rose	1883	foliage of beautiful red color in spring, flowers of saffron orange, tea-rose scent
'The Bride'	Tea	1869	white version of Catherine Mermet
'Ulrich Brunner Fils'	Hybrid Perpetual	1881	bright cerise red, very large and full of magnificent petals

CREATING A VICTORIAN BOUQUET

Any kind of flower arranging takes practice and patience. Rebecca Cole of Cole Creates in New York City has these instructions for building a beautiful bouquet.

1. Choose a number of different kinds of flowers for your bouquet.

- Tea roses were very popular as the centerpiece of a Victorian bouquet.
- Consider lemon-scented verbena, sweetbrier, and myrtle as the other components.
- Cut an odd number of every kind of flower.
- Keep as tight a color palette as possible.
- An effective bouquet will also have a variety of textures. Look for different kinds of flowers and other ornaments like berries.
- A big bouquet might include twenty-five flowers so make sure the stems are not too thick.
- Don't forget plenty of foliage. Fern and other plants with interesting leaves are good choices.

2. Use a very sharp, clean pair of pruners when cutting the flowers from your garden. You do not want to squeeze the stems.

3. Once brought inside the house, cut the stems again at a very sharp angle and put them in a vase of room-temperature water for at least an hour. The water should contain a commercial flower freshener or bleach ($^1/_2$ teaspoon per gallon) to prevent mold and bacteria from setting in.

- Cut off as many leaves as you can. No leaves should be submerged in the water, and the fewer leaves left on the stem, the longer the bloom will last.
- If the flowers have started to wilt already, shock them by submerging them for a minute in really hot water.
- Flowers that bleed any kind of milky sap when cut must be cauterized. Burn the very tip of the stem with a candle or dip it quickly in scalding hot water.
- Narcissus must be kept separate from other flowers for at least twenty-four hours as they emit a substance that will cause the others to wilt.

4. Keep the flowers out of the sun and as cool as possible until you are ready to construct the bouquet. Some people like to refrigerate them, but a word to the wise: While temperature found in most refrigerators is OK, some fruits emit a gas that will cause your flowers to wilt, so keep flowers and produce separate.

Making the Bouquet

1. Cut the stems so that there will be about 2 inches showing below your hands. The stems will get cut again before you finish.

2. As you build, hold the bouquet in one hand, adding flowers with the other. Some people find it useful to stand in front of a mirror so they can see how the arrangement will look on all sides.

3. Take three of your center flowers, put them together in one hand, and lay foliage between them.

4. Twist the arrangement in your hand and add two more central blooms if you want, remembering to layer in foliage.

Make sure that the first original three center pieces remain higher in the arrangement than the others.

5. Add your secondary flowers next, including foliage. Don't arrange them evenly. It looks more natural if, for example, you put three blooms on one side and two on the other. Continue building with all of the flowers, making sure that each layer is a bit lower than the previous one.

6. Use only foliage as the last layer.

7. Look at the arrangement carefully and make adjustments as needed.

8. Bind together tightly all of the stems using floral tape. Floral wire is OK, but it may cut into your plants. Start wrapping from just below the lowest flower and continue down the stems for an inch or so.

9. Take 5 feet of ribbon, lay it out on a table, and place the flowers in the middle of it. Tightly wrap the ribbon around the bouquet by crisscrossing it from both sides. Make sure you cover all of the floral tape and continue down the stems for 2 more inches. Tie it off well, using the two ends for a bow.

10. Cut off the stems to 1 inch below the ribbon.

11. Store the bouquet in a vase or jar of water that will support the flowers while allowing just the ends of the stems (not the ribbon) to touch the water.

While the process is not complicated, doing it well takes some experimentation, so be sure to try some practice runs before any special occasion.

PLANTSPEAK, OR THE LANGUAGE OF FLOWERS

In the nineteenth century, ascribing meanings to flowers became a popular pastime. These associations were derived from the inherent qualities of the flower, such as its color, fragrance, growth habit, or habitat. Burdock, for example, symbolized importunity because its seeds often stuck to clothing and it was difficult to remove. Literary and classical mythology were additional sources of inspiration. Narcissus, for example, represented egotism and self-love.

Using flowers alone, ladies (and gentlemen) could telegraph short messages or thoughts for nearly every occasion. In particular, the floral language was viewed as ideal for communicating the various facets of love, emotions that could not always be expressed within the rules of social decorum. A red rose was, and still is, a symbol of love and beauty, but red and white together signified scandal. A yellow rose was the badge of infidelity. The recipient could also send a message depending on where she wore the flower. By wearing the flower near her heart, a young woman declared her true love. If the flower was worn at the waist, she expressed interest, but no commitment. If she placed it in her hair, watch out! The message was clearly, "Stay away!"

Here are some other flowers and their Victorian connotations:

Amaranth	immortality
Amaryllis	pride, haughtiness
Anemone	forsaken love
Bluebell	delicacy, kindness
Buttercup	cheerfulness
Carnation	disdain
Clematis	beauty of mind
Crocus	youth
Dahlia	elegance and dignity
Fennel	strength
Hollyhock	ambition
Honeysuckle	affection
Hyacinth	constancy
Jasmine	amiability
Lady's Slipper	capricious beauty
Lavender	distrust
Lilac	first love
Lily of the Valley	modesty
Marigold	grief
Mignonette	your qualities surpass your charms
Moss	maternal love
Moss rose	confession of love
Myrtle	love
Pansy	think of me
Peony	anger
Pink	pure love
Poppy	consolation
Rose, red	beauty and love
Rose, white	I prefer to be single
Rose, yellow	jealousy
Rosemary	remembrance
Scarlet Geranium	stupidity
Snowdrop	hope
Sunflower	false riches
Thyme	activity
Tuberose	dangerous love
Tulip	declaration of love
Violet	modest worth

The frequency with which Caroline hosted afternoon teas (nearly every day) would be impossible for most working women today. But a Victorian tea party is a great way to gather family and friends for a special occasion or to shower a prospective mother or a bride-to-be. If you have a beautiful garden to serve as the setting, all the better. Here are some tips for a successful tea:

• Handwritten invitations are almost de rigueur, and in this day and age of E-mail, they really stand out. Send them out at least two weeks in advance.

• Pick a weekend afternoon for tea when the guests will have time to relax and enjoy.

• Teatime should last two to three hours. Mid- to late afternoon is appropriate, but remember that, traditionally, the later your party, the more substantial the food must be.

• While you might not be willing to risk your grandmother's antique china in the backyard, the cups, saucers, plates, and serving trays used during afternoon teas are traditionally very fancy. Perhaps you can find an inexpensive but delicate and elegant-looking setting at a yard sale or in a thrift shop. Crisply folded cloth napkins are a must.

• For decorations, indoors or out, consider filling extra teacups or teapots with cut flowers. You can adorn tables with potted plants; just make sure the pots are decorative enough for the occasion. Plain terracotta will not do.

• Furniture should include a large cloth-covered table, a separate smaller table for the tea service, and a group of comfortable chairs.

• A proper service includes an assortment of teas, perhaps one black, one blend, and one herbal. Make sure you have a bowl of sugar, preferably lump sugar, with appropriate tongs, a dish of thin lemon wedges, and a pitcher of milk. It might be wise to consider a second beverage for those who are not tea drinkers. Try punch, champagne, or sparkling water.

• Sandwiches are a tea-party must. Consider these traditional favorites: cucumber and butter on white bread, an O'Reilly favorite; egg salad or curried chicken salad on wheat bread; or smoked salmon on rye. Be sure to cut the sandwiches into small portions. Bread quarters traditionally with the crust removed, work well.

• Tea and scones are almost a cliché since they go so well together! The simple, light biscuits are served with jam. Caroline made her own strawberry, raspberry, and currant jams.

• For sweets, lemon-curd tart was a regular at Point Ellice parties. Also appropriate are sugar cookies or cupcakes.

• The hostess usually has the honor of pouring the tea.

Mrs. O'Reilly's Tea Party Favorites

For very special occasions, a formal tea party at Point Ellice might feature a richly varied menu. More commonly, however, the gatherings were more intimate—just immediate family or dear friends. For them, Caroline would put out her homemade jams, spread on freshly baked bread, or perhaps some of her favorite pastries.

Here are some recipes for tea-party favorites taken directly from Caroline O'Reilly's cookbooks. Given the fact that her directions were sometimes a bit vague, not to mention changes in acceptable degrees of sweetness and the like over the last 120 years, you may want to experiment in advance with these recipes in your own kitchen before serving them to guests.

Tea Cakes

3 cups white sugar
3 eggs
1 cup butter
1 cup milk
1 teaspoon baking soda
4 cups of sifted flour

Beat all ingredients well. Bake in shallow tins. Flavor to taste.

Brown Cake

1 pound flour
1 pound mixed fruit
$^1/_2$ pound butter
$^3/_4$ brown sugar [Caroline does indicate whether this is pound or cup measure]
3 eggs
4 teaspoons mixed spice
a little salt and a little warm milk
l large teaspoon baking soda

Beat all ingredients well. Bake in a quick oven for about 2 hours. A few cherries added keeps it moist.

Sponge Cake

1 cup flour
1 cup sifted sugar
1 teaspoon cream of tartar
3 eggs, well beaten
$^1/_2$ cup milk
$^1/_2$ teaspoon carbonate of soda
a little essence [vanilla or almond flavoring]

Mix together the flour, sugar, and tartar and pass through a sieve. Gradually add the eggs until all of the flour has been soaked up. Add the milk and soda. Flavor with a little essence. Pour into a tin that's "not too deep" and bake in "a rather quick oven" [high temperature], taking care there is more heat at the bottom of the oven than at the top.

Good Plain Cake

1 pound flour
2 teaspoons baking powder
a pinch of salt and spice
$^1/_4$ pound sugar
$^1/_4$ pound butter
6 ounces sultanas [yellow raisins]
2 ounces currants [dried]
1 ounce candied peel
2 eggs, beaten
half a teacupful of milk

Mix ingredients well together and bake well in a quick [high temperature] oven.

Raspberry Pudding

[Caroline used berries from her gardens to make raspberry, strawberry, and currant jams. And she frequently used those jams in her tea-party recipes. This pudding was probably such a common dish that she needed only the barest of notes to remember how to create it.]

Mix together 2 eggs, "their weight in flour," butter, white sifted sugar, 2 tablespoons of raspberry jam, and $^1/_2$ teaspoon of carbonate of soda. Boil for 2 hours. "Serve with wine sauce." [A dinnertime dessert.]

Russian Sticks

$^1/_4$ pound cheese
$^1/_4$ pound flour
$^1/_4$ pound butter
Cayenne pepper

Grate the cheese and mix with the other ingredients. Roll up and cut into long strips. Bake in "a quick oven [high temperature]. They should be eaten while warm." [Savories might be served for a late tea, not afternoon tea stuff.]

Lemon Cheese Cakes [Lemon Curd]

$^1/_4$ pound butter
1 pound sugar
6 eggs
rinds from 2 lemons [grated]
juice from 3 lemons [strained]

Put all of the ingredients into a stew pan. Keep stirring the mixture until the sugar is dissolved and it begins to thicken. When it is the consistency of honey, it is done. (Lemon curd is the filling for the lemon tarts.)

Paste for Custards

[*Custard* is the nineteenth-century term for baked goods such as tarts. *Paste* refers to pastry or pie crust.]

6 ounces butter
$^1/_2$ pound flour
2 egg yolks
3 tablespoons cream

Rub butter into the flour. Mix it well together with the egg yolks and the cream. Let it stand for a quarter of an hour; then work it up, and roll it out very thin for use.

Very Rich Short Crust

10 ounces butter
1 pound flour
a pinch of salt
2 ounces loaf sugar
2 eggs, beaten
a little milk

Break butter into the flour dried and sifted. Add the salt and the sugar rolled fine. Make it into a very smooth paste as lightly as possible, with the eggs, and sufficient milk to moisten the paste.

PLAYING CROQUET THE VICTORIAN WAY

While no longer quite the ubiquitous pastime it once was, croquet is an amusing and civilized way to pass an hour or two with friends. All that's needed to relive this Victorian pleasure is a level stretch of lawn, a croquet set, and a competitive spirit. The rules below come from the United States Croquet Association (www.croquetamerica.com) and are especially adapted for home play. They do bear reading, however, as even those of us who played as children will probably find we have been bending a rule or two!

Game Overview

The standard double-diamond rectangular court officially measuring 50 feet wide and 100 feet long may be reduced to fit the size and shape of the space available. If you reduce the court, try to maintain a 6-foot separation between the Starting/Turning stake and the adjacent wickets; a shorter distance constricts the playing space and affects game tactics.

The game is designed for up to six balls, and may be played with any number of players from two to six. There are always either four balls (two on each side) or six balls (three on each side).

A game usually requires from one to two hours to play to its conclusion; that is, until one of the players or teams has "staked out" by scoring all the wickets and striking the Finishing Stake with all the balls on its side.

The Sides

There are always only two sides, with the "hot colors" (red/yellow/orange) competing against the "cool colors" (blue/black/green). When only four balls are played, the sides are blue/black against red/yellow.

The Players

Croquet may be played with 2, 3, 4, 5, or 6 players. When the number of players equals the number of balls on a side, each player plays only one ball throughout the game. When the number of players does not equal the number of balls on a side, the players on that side alternate turns and may play any one ball on their side in a turn. Team captains may be chosen, and players may confer to decide which ball should be played in each turn. With two players, each of them plays all the balls on a side.

Starting the Game

A coin toss gives the winning side the choice of playing first or second. Each of the balls must be brought into play in the first round of turns, in the order of the colors on the stake: blue/red/black/yellow/green/orange. The starting "tee" is one mallet length in front of Wicket #1.

The Turn

A turn consists of one stroke plus any additional bonus strokes earned by the ball in play. After the first round of turns, a side may play any one of its balls in each turn.

At the conclusion of a turn in which a wicket or stake point is scored, the wicket clip of the color corresponding to the ball should be placed on the next wicket or stake to be scored by that ball. If your set does not include wicket clips, you may use colored clothespins.

Bonus Strokes

There are two ways to earn bonus strokes: by scoring wicket and stake points or by hitting (also called roqueting) an opponent's ball with the ball in play.

Wicket or Stake Bonus Stroke: One bonus stroke is earned for passing through your proper wicket in the order of the course. One bonus stroke is earned for striking the Turning Stake after scoring Wicket #7. These strokes must be played from where the ball lies after the point is made. No bonus stroke is earned by a ball that "pegs out" by striking the Finishing Stake.

Roquet Bonus Stroke: You get two bonus strokes when your ball hits (or roquets) a ball of the other side.

The Croquet Stroke is the first of these,

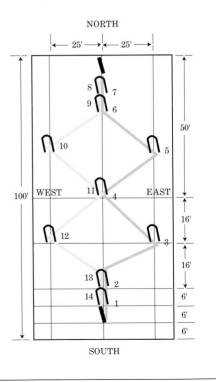

played either in contact with the roqueted ball or from one mallet head's distance. The contact Croquet Stroke is played by placing your ball in contact with the ball you hit (roqueted) and striking your ball to make both your ball (the striker's ball) and the other ball (the roqueted ball) move. If you wish, you may place your foot on top of your ball to keep it in place while you strike it, sending the roqueted ball in the desired direction.

Note: You may choose to outlaw contact Croquet Strokes to help equalize playing levels and prevent stronger players from dominating the game.

The Continuation Stroke is the second of the two roquet bonus strokes. It is played from wherever the striker's ball lies after the Croquet Stroke. At the beginning of every turn, a player is eligible to roquet any opponent ball(s). Each opponent ball may be roqueted for bonus strokes only once in a turn unless the striker scores a wicket (or the Turning Stake). Scoring a point entitles the striker to roquet each of the opponent balls again, and a skillful player may score several wickets in one turn.

Bonus strokes may not be accumulated. Only the last-earned bonus stroke(s) may be played. On the Croquet Stroke, if the striker's ball clears a wicket, the Continuation Stroke is lost, and only the Wicket Bonus Stroke may be played. On the Croquet Stroke, if the striker's ball roquets another ball on which it is entitled to take bonus strokes, the Continuation Stroke from the first roquet is lost, and you are entitled only to the two newly earned bonus strokes.

If your ball clears a wicket and in the same stroke hits an opponent ball on the other side of the wicket, the hit does not count as a roquet; you may, however, then choose to roquet the opponent ball with your Wicket Bonus Stroke.

There is one exception to the rule against accumulating bonus strokes. You may earn two bonus strokes by scoring two wickets in one stroke. This commonly occurs at the Starting Stake and the Turning Stake, when you may score both wickets in one stroke so you can use the two consecutive bonus strokes earned to attack the position of the other side(s).

If another player sends your ball through its proper wicket, or into its stake, your ball does score the point; however, there is no bonus stroke. Bonus strokes may be earned only by the ball in play during its own turn.

Rover Balls

Rovers are balls that have completed all the course except for striking the Finishing Stake. Rovers may be staked out (driven into the Finishing Stake) with any legal stroke by any player at any point in the game.

Winning the Game

The side that scores all the wickets and strikes the Finishing Stake with all its balls wins the game. In timed games, the side with the most points wins when time is called; each wicket or stake scored by each ball counts for a point. If there is a tie, keep playing until one side scores a point and thus wins the game.

Boundaries

String or other marked boundaries for the nine-wicket court shown in the illustration are not essential. Natural boundaries such as a sidewalk, a precipitous cliff, the surf line, or the neighbor's petunia bed will work as well. To forestall disputes, make specific agreements on boundaries before starting.

Boundaries designated by a string or special markings should be at least 6 feet beyond the outer wickets and stakes.

Boundary Balls

All balls sent out of bounds are brought to the point where they crossed the designated boundary and placed one mallet length inside the court before play resumes. There is no penalty or loss of strokes for sending any ball out of bounds. Out-of-bounds balls are simply placed in bounds, and play resumes. All balls that come to rest within the Boundary Margin (closer than a mallet-length to the boundary) are immediately replaced on the Boundary Margin, with the one exception of the striker's ball still in play on a Continuation Stroke or a Wicket Bonus Stroke, which is played from wherever it lies within the Boundary Margin.

Faults and Penalties

You must strike the ball only with the face of the mallet. The mallet may not touch any other ball except the striker's, nor may it strike a wicket or stake, nor may it "crush" a ball against a wicket or stake to make the wicket or stake bend or move.

There are no penalties for faults. Out-of-turn plays and all faults should be corrected by replacing the balls to their positions before the fault occurred and replaying the shots correctly.

Unless there is a previously appointed referee, the word of the striker should be accepted in disputes. In disagreements on replacement of balls to replay fouled strokes, the offending side must accept the judgment of the opponent.

Take a close look at the historic photos of the Point Ellice kitchen garden, and you'll see an intriguing fencelike structure running down the side of the main north-south path. Victorian gardeners would have instantly identified this as a support for espaliered fruit trees, although most modern gardeners wouldn't be so quick to do so; espaliers have become something of a lost art. That's really too bad because, in this day and age of ever-decreasing garden size and greater and greater demand for more from less, the ancient practice of espalier is a wonderfully simple way to increase the beauty, and the bounty, of your garden.

Espalier refers to the custom of training shrubs and trees to grow flat against a wall, fence, or other freestanding divider. The practice seems to have originated with the Romans, and has been used ever since by anyone interested in making the most of their gardening space. Although many purely ornamental plants can be used to create the decorative espalier patterns, it is with fruit trees, such as apples and pears, that the practice really comes to fruition, if you'll pardon the pun. The severe pruning and training required to shape an espalier also happens to promote the growth of "spurs," the special branches on which the fruit forms. The more spurs you have, the more apples or pears you'll get, and even a relatively small, 5 to 6 foot espalier can bear as much or more than a standard dwarf tree.

Starting an espalier is not difficult. All that's required is a bit of planning, a little elbow grease, and a not inconsiderable amount of patience. It often takes three to five years, or more, for an espalier to reach maturity. The beauty of the completed project, though, is certainly worth the wait. The first step in the process is to decide just what type of espalier you want. There are many different design possibilities: a simple cordon, or straight line, which can be run vertically or obliquely on an angle with several other plants to form a pattern of interlocking diamonds; a candelabra or palmette verrier, named after the famous nineteenth-century French master gardener who perfected the technique; a horizontal T, also called a tier; or a fan.

Once you decide on a shape, the next step is prepare the framework. While it is possible to train an espalier directly onto a wall or solid fence using specially made nails (commonly called rose hooks) that have a strip of flexible lead at the top to catch and hold the branches, it's much easier to start your espalier on a wire or lattice framework, such as the simple rustic supports used at Point Ellice. To establish the framework, take two posts as tall as your intended espalier and spread the posts as far apart as you want your espalier to grow. Make sure of course that if you are using wood, it is rot resistant.

Between the posts, string three to five strands of heavy galvanized wire and tighten until completely taught. If possible, try to make sure your line of espalier runs north to south for maximum light (one-sided espaliers, such as those on solid walls, should face south). Fruit trees especially, when backed by a south-facing wall, will appreciate the extra warmth when it is time to mature the crop.

Next choose your plant. For fruit trees, its best to use one- or two-year-old whips (young plants) that have been grafted onto dwarf stock. Their diminutive size will help to keep them in check later. For other ornamentals, try to find a specimen whose branches already more or less correspond to the pattern you intend, a challenging, but not impossible task. Place the plant in the center of the sup-

ports. The next step will depend upon whether or not your young plant has many branches. If well limbed, take sharp pruners and trim away all those that don't conform to your intended pattern and secure those that do with soft bindings that won't cut into the bark. Believe it or not, cut-up strips of old nylon stockings are terrific for this; for the hose-less, yarn or any other soft, natural string will work. For plants that have minimal branches, remove any that don't conform to your design, tie up those that do, then wait. As new branches appear, remove those you don't want, and slowly bend and attach those you do onto the wire framework. A certain amount of pinching back may also be involved, depending on your final plan. The exact process varies slightly with each type of design, and a good book, such

as *Taylor's Weekend Gardening Guide to Topiaries and Espalier*, 1999, will show you quickly and easily how to form the various patterns.

Besides the already-mentioned apples and pears, peaches, oranges, nectarines, pomegranates, kumquats, limes, lemons, and quinces all make excellent candidates for productive espaliers. For purely ornamental purposes, plants with berries, such as crab apples and pyracantha (*Pyracantha coccinea*) are excellent. Oleander (*Nerium oleander*), winged burning bush (*Euonymus alata*), Japanese holly (*Ilex crenata*), hibiscus (*Hibiscus rosasinensis*), and common yews (*Taxus* spp.) can also be effectively espaliered. Just be sure to check out the plant's hardiness and other general requirements before you proceed.

NATURALIZING BULBS

There is perhaps no more suitable candidate for the wild garden than spring bulbs. All the negative factors that plague bulbs in the perennial border—the difficulty of correctly sequencing bloom, wide differences in flowering height, the unsightliness of decaying foliage after flowering—none of these are an issue when bulbs are left to naturalize in a wild setting. Most bulbs common to the border, with the notable exception of standard tulips, are perfect for this usage: snowdrops, daffodils, bluebells, and many others (see the list below). All emerge before the trees leaf out and other competing plants are able to overtake them. In this way they receive enough light to flower happily for weeks, lighting up the empty woodlands with color. Then as the foliage of the trees and undergrowth appears, they gracefully fade into the background, to wait their turn on stage again the following spring. Best of all, this magnificent show occurs without the intervention of the gardener, save for the initial planting. Although digging in a wooded setting among tree roots can often be a fairly laborious enterprise, once properly planted, naturalized bulbs will bloom for decades. Here are a few tips to ensure success:

1. Be sure to choose bulbs that bloom early to midspring, giving the plant sufficient time to store energy for next year's bloom before the foliage canopy limits the light. Among these are almost all of the early daffodils and narcissi, including the dwarf forms; snowdrops (*Galanthus* spp.); squill (*Scilla* spp.); crocuses (*Crocus* spp.); grape hyacinths (*Muscari* spp.); hardy cyclamen (*Cyclamen cilicium*); pushkinia (*Pushkinia libanotica*), and the fritillaries (*Fritillaria* spp.). Most tulips, with the exception of the tiny, early botanical species like *T. tarda* and *humilis*, are not good choices, for their fairly formal appearance clashes with the relaxed feeling of the wild garden, not to mention the fact that modern hybridization has essentially removed the perennial nature of these bulbs, requiring the gardener to replant each year. Late-spring and early summer bloomers, such as late daffodils and most of the lilies, should only be planted in more open settings or on the margins of wooded areas where they will receive sufficient light to mature their foliage.

2. Unlike the perennial border where spacing instructions can be ignored and bulbs can be planted close together to produce dense clumps, in the woodland garden bulbs should be planted according to individual instructions with a generous handful of fertilizer or bone-meal in each hole, to compensate for the competition from established trees and shrub roots. This extra burst of fertilizer, along with the more ample spacing, will help the bulb to settle happily into its new home. While the effect in the first year will be somewhat less full, longevity and bloom will be increased substantially, and the bulbs will form far more naturalistic drifts and clumps when left to their own devices.

3. Digging among tree and shrub roots can often be a notoriously arduous affair, and there will always be a temptation to give up and plant the bulbs more shallowly than required. Instead, try this. If the spot you have chosen can't be dug to a sufficient depth, simply select another and start again. Once you have found a more forgiving location, you can make up any lost effort by layering several species bulbs in a single, ample hole. Simply plant the bulbs requiring the greatest depth and latest blooming times first—let's use large-flowered, midseason daffodils, planted 8 inches deep, as an example. Throw in a handful of fertilizer and cover them with a few inches of soil. Then plant some of the earlier, smaller narcissus varieties, which bloom in early spring and require about 5 inches of soil; finally, after adding a touch more fertilizer and an inch or two of soil, place some very early giant crocus, snowdrops, or muscari on top. Fertilize and cover. Each and every hole will now produce a succession of blooms for well over a month.

128

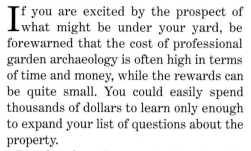

If you are excited by the prospect of what might be under your yard, be forewarned that the cost of professional garden archaeology is often high in terms of time and money, while the rewards can be quite small. You could easily spend thousands of dollars to learn only enough to expand your list of questions about the property.

But that doesn't mean that the inquisitive garden historian needs to remain totally in the dark. Here are some tips for piecing together the story of your land, without hiring an expert.

• Trace the legal history of your property as far back as you can. Records are kept at most city or county registrar's offices. Make a time line of who owned the property and when. Keep an eye out for land surveys that might indicate the location of fences, walkways, and outbuildings.

• Check with local historical societies and try to find pictures of your home. Newspapers may also have recorded and described social events such as weddings held there.

• Track down the families of previous owners and talk to your neighbors. Ask them about pictures or memories they have. Someone may recall the controversy created by a new driveway or the brouhaha caused by a tennis ball being batted into a prized patch of petunias.

• Try to track down the maker and manufacture date of any old pots, bottles, or even bricks that you find. Old catalogs, books, or the Internet can help you date old tools and the fortunes of the companies that made them.

• Keep your eyes open at local antique shops and flea markets for items similar to any artifacts you may have unearthed. A single old pot, for example, can often be mated with store-bought finds, or old tools recombined to form complete sets.

• For owners of houses with particular historical interest, you may want to contact your local university and find out whether or not course work in archaeology is offered. If it is, and if your site is sufficiently unique historically, the university may wish to use your garden for an educational dig, providing you with low-cost answers to your questions, as well as valuable learning opportunities for archaeologists in training.

KITCHEN GARDEN RECIPES

Modern Versions of Vegetable Recipes from Caroline's Kitchen

Pea Soup

1 small onion, sliced
1 tablespoon oil
2 cups shelled peas
$^1/_2$ cup lettuce
2 tablespoons chopped mint
2 cups chicken or vegetable stock
2 egg yolks mixed with 1 cup milk

In a large pot, sauté the onion in the oil until it is golden. Add the peas, lettuce, mint, stock, and egg mixture. Bring to a boil, then reduce the heat and let simmer until the peas are soft but not falling apart. Puree in a food processor. Return to the pot and reheat. Serve with croutons.

Tomato Chutney

2 pounds tomatoes
2 shallots or small onions
$^1/_2$ pound peeled and boiled apples
$^1/_2$ pound raisins
2 teaspoons powered ginger
2 dried chili peppers
1 clove finely shredded garlic
1 cup cider vinegar

Peel and slice the tomatoes and onions. Chop the cooked apples into small pieces. In a large stainless-steel pot, mix together all of the remaining ingredients. Bring to a boil, stirring frequently. Reduce the heat and simmer, uncovered, for about 3 hours until the chutney is thick and rich in color.

Scalloped Cauliflower

1 head cauliflower
$^1/_2$ teaspoon butter
$^1/_4$ cup bread crumbs
$^3/_4$ cup milk or half-and-half
$^1/_2$ cup shredded cheddar cheese
salt and cayenne pepper

Preheat the oven to 350°F. Break the cauliflower into florets and steam until tender. Drain. In a separate saucepan, melt the butter. Mix in the bread crumbs, milk, cheese, and salt and pepper. Stir until thick but pourable. Put the cauliflower pieces in a baking dish. Pour the contents of the saucepan over the pieces. Bake for 10–15 minutes or until the sauce bubbles.

Raspberry Pudding

2 cups fresh raspberries
$^1/_2$ cup sugar
2 tablespoons cornstarch
1 egg
$^1/_2$ teaspoon baking soda

In a large saucepan, mash the raspberries. Stir in the sugar, cornstarch, egg, and baking soda. Cook over medium heat, stirring constantly, until thick and bubbly. Allow to cool. Cover and chill for 2 hours.

BIBLIOGRAPHY

Adams, William H. *Grounds for Change: Major Gardens of the Twentieth Century.* Boston: Bulfinch Press, 1993.

———. *Nature Perfected: Gardens Through History.* New York: Abbeville Press, 1991.

Appleton, Bonnie Lee. *Landscape Rejuvenation.* Pownal, VT: Storey Communications, 1988.

Arthurs Karthryn, ed. *Terrariums and Miniature Gardens.* Menlo Park, CA: Lane Books, 1973.

Bailey, L.H. *The Nursery Book.* London: Macmillan, 1907.

———. The Rural Science Series: *The Nursery Book.* New York: Macmillan, 1907.

Bailey Hortorium. *Hortus Third: A Concise Dictionary of Plants Cultivated in the United States and Canada.* New York: John Wiley & Sons, 1976.

Beecher, Catharine. *Miss Beecher's Domestic Receipt Book: Designed as a Supplement to Her Treatis on Domestic Economy.* New York: Harper and Collins, 1858.

Benjamin, Asher. *The American Builder's Companion.* New York: Dover Publications, 1969.

Bickford-Swart, Doris. *The Best of Times: 1870–1915. Heritage Gardening at Cradle Knoll Farm.* Deansboro, NY: Berry Hill Press, 1998.

Billington, Jill. *Architectural Foliage: Shape, Form and Texture of Foliage Plants in Garden Design.* London: Ward Lock, 1991.

Blomfield, Reginald, and F. Inigo Thomas. *The Formal Garden in England.* London: Macmillan, 1892.

Boggs, Kate Doggett. *Prints and Plants of Old Gardens.* Richmond: Garrett & Massie, 1932.

Boisset, Caroline. *Gardening in Time: Planning Future Growth and Flowering.* New York: Prentice Hall, 1990.

Bowles, E.A. *My Garden in Spring.* Portland, OR: Timber Press, 1997.

———. *My Garden in Summer.* Portland, OR: Timber Press, 1998.

Bowling, Barbara. *The Berry Grower's Companion.* Portland, OR: Timber Press, 2000.

Breck, Joseph. *The Flower Garden.* New York: John P. Jewett, 1856.

Brierton, Joan M. *Victorian: American Restoration Style.* Layton, UT: Gibbs Smith, 1999.

Brookes, John. *The Country Garden: A Seasonal Guide to Designing and Planting Gardens with Natural Style.* New York: Crown, 1987.

———. *The Gardener's Index of Plants & Flowers.* New York: Macmillan, 1987.

———. *The Small Garden Book.* New York: Crown, 1989.

Brown, Jane. *The Art and Architecture of English Gardens.* New York: Rizzoli, 1989.

———. *Sissinghurst: Portrait of a Garden.* New York: Abrams, 1990.

Buczacki, Stefan. *Creating a Victorian Flower Garden.* New York: Weidenfeld & Nicolson, 1988.

Burbidge, F.W. *Domestic Floriculture.* London: William Blackwood and Sons, 1874.

Burpee, F.W. *Burpee's Farm Annual.* Philadelphia: W. Atlee Burpee and Company, 1894.

Bynum, Flora Ann. *The Influence of Women on the Southern Landscape.* Winston-Salem, NC: Old Salem, 1997.

Charlton, James, and William Thompson. *Croquet: The Complete Guide to History, Strategy, Rules, and Records.* New York: Turtle Press, 1977.

Christopher, Thomas. *In Search of Lost Roses.* New York: Summit Books, 1989.

Cleaveland, Henry W., William Cleaveland, and Samuel Cleaveland. *Village and Farm Cottages.* New York: D. Appleton and Company, 1856.

Coats, Alice. *Flowers and Their Histories.* London: McGraw-Hill, 1968.

Coats, Alice M., and Dr. John L. Creech. *Garden Shrubs and Their Histories.* New York: Simon & Schuster, 1992.

Coffin, David R. *The English Garden: Meditation and Memorial.* Princeton: Princeton University Press, 1994.

Colborn, Nigel. *The Old-Fashioned Gardener: Lessons from the Past for the Gardener of Today.* London: Anness Publishing, 1995.

Copeland, Morris. *Country Life: A Handbook of Agriculture, Horticulture, and Landscape Gardening.* Boston: John P. Jewett, 1860.

Coughlin, Roberta M. *The Gardener's Companion: A Book of Lists and Lore.* New York: HarperCollins, 1991.

Cruso, Thalassa. *Making Things Grow Indoors.* New York: Alfred A. Knopf, 1977.

———. *Making Things Grow Outdoors.* New York: Alfred A. Knopf, 1976.

———. *Making Vegetables Grow.* New York: Alfred A. Knopf, 1975.

———. *To Everything There Is a Season: The Gardening Year.* New York: Alfred A. Knopf, 1974.

Culpeper, William. *Culpeper's Color Herbal.* New York: Sterling Publishing Company, 1983.

Curtis, Charles. *Orchids—Their Description and Cultivation.* London: Putnam & Company, 1950.

Davies, Jennifer. *The Victorian Flower Garden.* London: BBC Books, 1991.

———. *The Victorian Kitchen Garden.* London: BBC Books, 1987.

Davis, Brian. *The Gardener's Illustrated Encyclopedia of Trees & Shrubs: A Guide to More Than 2,000.* Emmaus, PA: Rodale Press, 1987.

Dirr, Michael A. *Dirr's Hardy Trees and Shrubs: An Illustrated Encyclopedia.* Portland, OR: Timber Press, 1997.

———. *Manual of Woody Landscape Plants.* Champaign, IL: Stipes Publishing Company, 1983.

Doell, M. Christine Klim. *Gardens of the Gilded Age: Nineteenth-Century Gardens and Home Grounds of New York State.* Syracuse, NY: Syracuse University Press, 1986.

Downing, Andrew. *Cottage Residences* (reprint of the 1873 edition). New York: Dover Publications, 1981.

———. *The Fruit and Fruit Trees of America.* New York: John Wiley & Sons, 1867.

Druse, Ken. *The Collector's Garden: Designing with Extraordinary Plants.* New York: Clarkson N. Potter, 1996.

Duncan, Frances. *Home Vegetables and Small Fruits.* New York: Charles Scribner's Sons, 1918.

Elder, Walter. *The Cottage Garden of America.* Philadelphia: Moss and Brother, 1850.

Elliott, Brent. *The Country House Garden: From the Archives of Country Life, 1897–1939.* London: Mitchell Beazley, 1995.

———. *Victorian Gardens.* Portland, OR: Timber Press, 1986.

Elliott, F.R. *Handbook of Practical Landscape Gardening.* Rochester, NY: D. M. Dewey, 1885.

Emmet, Alan. *So Fine a Prospect: Historic New England Gardens.* Hanover, NH: University Press of New England, 1996.

Favretti, Rudy J., and Joy P. Favretti. *For Every House a Garden.* Hanover, NH: University Press of New England, 1990.

———. *Landscapes and Gardens for Historic Buildings.* Nashville: American Association for State and Local History, 1991.

Galle, Fred C. *Hollies: The Genus Ilex.* Portland, OR: Timber Press, 1997.

Gardner, Jo Ann. *The Heirloom Garden: Selecting and Growing Over 300 Old-Fashioned Ornamentals.* Pownal, VT: Storey Communications, 1992.

Garnock, Jamie. *Trellis: The Creative Way to Transform Your Garden.* New York: Rizzoli, 1991.

Gertley, Jan, and Michael Gertley. *Classic Garden Structures: 18 Elegant Projects to Enhance Your Garden.* Newtown, CT: Taunton Press, 1998.

Fifty Years of Lawn Tennis in the United States. New York: United States Lawn Tennis Association, 1931.

Girouard, Mark. *The Victorian Country House.* New Haven, CT: Yale University Press, 1979.

Glattstein, Judy. *Garden Design with Foliage: Ferns and Grasses, Vines and Ground Covers, Annuals and Perennials.* Pownal, VT: Storey Communications, 1991.

Gothein, Marie Louise. *A History of Garden Art.* New York: Hacker Art Books, 1979.

Green, Harvey. *The Light of the Home: An Intimate View of the Lives of Women in Victorian America.* New York: Pantheon Books, 1983.

Greenberg, David B., ed. and Jack Wilson, ill. *Countryman's Companion.* New York: Harper & Brothers Publishers, 1947.

Grey-Wilson, Christopher, and Victoria Matthews. *Gardening with Climbers.* Portland, OR: Timber Press, 1997.

Grover, Kathryn. *Dining in America, 1850–1900.* Amherst, MA: University of Massachusetts Press, 1987.

Gunn, Fenja. *Lost Gardens of Gertrude Jekyll.* New York: Macmillan, 1991.

Hale, Jonathan. *The Old Way of Seeing: How Architec-ture Lost Its Magic (and How to Get It Back)* Boston: Houghton Mifflin Company, 1994.

Harris, Cyril M., ed. *Illustrated Dictionary of Historic Architecture.* New York: Dover Publications, 1977.

Harris, John, ed. *The Garden: A Celebration of One Thousand Years of British Gardening.* London: New Perspectives Publishing, 1979.

Hayward, Gordon. *Garden Paths: A New Way to Solve Practical Problems in the Garden.* Boston: Houghton Mifflin Company, 1998.

Heffner, Sarah. *Heirloom Country Gardens.* Emmaus, PA: Rodale Press, 1999.

Henderson, Peter. *Gardening for Pleasure.* New York: Orange Judd Company, 1893.

———. *Gardening for Profit.* New York: Orange Judd Company, 1908.

Hibberd, Shirley. *The Amateur's Flower Garden.* London: Groombridge and Sons, 1871.

———. *The Amateur's Rose Book.* London: Groombridge and Sons, 1874.

———. *The Fern Garden: How to Make, Keep and Enjoy It.* London: Groombridge and Sons, 1869.

———. *Profitable Gardening.* London: Groombridge and Sons, 1863.

———. *Rustic Adornments for Homes of Taste.* London: Groombridge and Sons, 1895.

Hill, Lewis. *Fruits and Berries for the Home Garden.* Pownal, VT: Storey Communications, 1992.

Hobhouse, Penelope. *Gardening Through the Ages: An Illustrated History of Plants and Their Influence on Garden Styles—from Ancient Egypt to the Present Day.* New York: Simon & Schuster, 1992.

———, ed. *Gertrude Jekyll on Gardening.* New York: Random House, 1985.

Holly, Henry. *Holly's Picturesque Country Seats: A Complete Reprint of the 1863 Classic.* New York: Dover Publications, 1993.

Hunt, John Dixon. *Gardens and the Picturesque: Studies in the History of Landscape Architecture.* Cambridge, MA: MIT Press, 1992.

Jekyll, Gertrude. *The Illustrated Gertrude Jekyll.* Boston: Little, Brown and Company, 1988.

Jekyll, Gertrude, and Lawrence Weaver. *Arts and Crafts Gardens*. Suffolk, UK: Garden Art Press, 1981.

———. *Gardens for Small Country Houses*. Suffolk, UK: Antique Collectors' Club, 1981.

Joyce, David. *Garden Styles: An Illustrated History of Design and Tradition*. London: Octopus, 1989.

Kaspar, Susanne. *The Great Book of Pears*. Berkeley: Ten Speed Press, 2000.

Kellaway, Herbert J. *How to Lay Out Suburban Home Grounds*. New York: John Wiley & Sons, 1915.

Kelso, William M., and Rachel Most, eds. *Earth Patterns: Essays in Landscape Archaeology*. Charlottesville, VA: University of Virginia Press, 1990.

Kemp, Edward. Edited by F. A. Waugh. *Landscape Gardening: How to Lay Out a Small Garden* (revised from the 1858 edition). New York: John Wiley & Sons, 1911.

Kowalczewski, Jan. *Garden Touring in the Pacific Northwest*. Seattle: Alaska Northwest Books, 1993.

Kylloe, Ralph. *Rustic Garden Architecture*. Salt Lake City: Gibbs Smith, 1997.

Lasdun, Susan. *The English Park: Royal, Private and Public*. New York: Vendome Press, 1992.

———. *Victorians at Home*. New York: Viking Press, 1981.

Lawson-Hall, Toni, and Brian Rothera. *Hydrangeas: A Gardener's Guide*. Portland, OR: Timber Press, 1996.

Ledward, Daphne. *The Victorian Garden Catalogue: A Treasure Trove of Horticultural Paraphernalia*. London: Studio Editions, 1995.

Leman, Anne M. *Fifty Easy Old-Fashioned Roses, Climbers, and Vines*. New York: Henry Holt and Company, 1995.

Lennox-Boyd, Arabella, and Clay Perry. *Traditional English Gardens*. London: Weidenfeld and Nicolson, 1987.

Leopold, Allison Kyle. *The Victorian Garden*. New York: Clarkson N. Potter, 1995.

———. *Victorian Splendor: Recreating America's 19th Century Interiors*. New York: Stewart, Tabori and Chang, 1986.

Lewis, Arnold. *American Country Houses of the Gilded Age*. New York: Dover Publications, 1982.

Lloyd, Christopher, and Richard Bird. *The Cottage Garden*. New York: Prentice Hall, 1990.

Long, Elias A. *Ornamental Gardening for Americans*. New York: Orange Judd Company, 1896.

Loudon, Jane Webb. *Ladies' Companion to the Flower Garden*. New York: John Wiley, 1853.

Martin, Tovah. *Heirloom Flowers: Vintage Flowers for Modern Gardens*. New York: Simon & Schuster, 1999.

———. *Window Boxes: How to Paint and Maintain Beautiful Compact Flower Beds*. Boston: Houghton Mifflin Company, 1997.

Mawe, Thomas, and John Abercrombie. *The Complete Gardener*. London: 1832.

———. *Mawe's Every Man His Own Gardener*. London: Griffin and Co., 1839.

Maynard, Samuel T. *Landscape Gardening as Applied to Home Decoration*. New York: John Wiley & Sons, 1903.

McMahon, Bernard. *The American Gardener's Calendar*. Charlottesville, VA: Thomas Jefferson, 1997.

Mitchell, Donald G. *Rural Studies*. New York: Charles Scribner and Company, 1867.

Mohlenbrock, Robert H. *Wildflowers: A Quick Identification Guide to the Wildflowers of North America*. New York: Macmillan, 1987.

Morris, Alistair. *Antiques from the Garden*. Wappingers Falls, NY: Garden Art Press, 1996.

Morse, Harriet K. *Gardening in the Shade*. Portland, OR: Timber Press, 1982.

Mosser, Monique, and Georges Teyssot, eds. *The Architecture of Western Gardens*. Cambridge, MA: MIT Press, 1991.

Murphy, Wendy B. *Beds and Borders: Traditional and Original Garden Designs*. Boston: Houghton Mifflin Company, 1990.

Newhall, Charles S. *The Shrubs of North-Eastern America*. New York: G. P. Putnam's Sons, 1893.

Nitschke, Robert. *Choice and Unusual Fruits for the Connoisseur and Home Gardener*. Lakeside, MI: Southmeadow Fruit Gardens, 1976.

Ottewill, David. *The Edwardian Garden*. New Haven:

Yale University Press, 1989.

Otto, Stella. *The Backyard Berry Book*. Maple City, MI: OttoGraphics, 1995.

———. *The Backyard Orchardist*. Maple City, MI: Otto-Graphics, 1993.

Parsons, Samuel. *Landscape Gardening*. New York: G. P. Putnam's Sons, 1891.

Platt, Charles A., and Keith N. Morgan. *Italian Gardens*. Portland, OR: Timber Press, 1993.

Practical Guide to Home Landscaping. Pleasantville, NY: The Reader's Digest Association, 1972.

Punch, Walter T., ed. *Keeping Eden: A History of Gardening in America*. Boston: Little, Brown and Company, 1992.

Rand, Edward Sprague, Jr. *Flowers for the Parlor and Garden*. Boston: J. E. Tilton and Co., 1864.

Reich, Lee. *Uncommon Fruits Worthy of Attention: A Gardener's Guide*. Reading, MA: Addison-Wesley Publishing, 1991.

Rice, Graham. *Plants for Problem Places*. Portland, OR: Timber Press, 1988.

Rickard, Martin. *The Plantfinder's Guide to Garden Ferns*. Portland, OR: Timber Press, 2000.

Robbins, Mary. *The Rescue of an Old Place*. Cambridge, MA: The Riverside Press, 1892.

Robinson, William. *The English Flower Garden*. Sagaponack, NY: Sagapress, 1995.

———. *The Wild Garden*. New York: Scribner and Welford, 1881.

Rogers, Ruth, and Nicholas H. Ekstrom. *Perennials for American Gardens*. New York: Random House, 1989.

Rutherford Ely, Helena. *A Woman's Hardy Garden*. New York: Macmillan, 1903.

Sackville-West, Victoria. *The Illustrated Garden Book*. New York: Atheneum, 1986.

———. *A Joy of Gardening*. New York: Harper and Row, 1958.

Sandler, Martin W. *This Was America*. Boston: Little, Brown and Company, 1980.

Schlereth, Thomas. *Victorian America: Transformations in Everyday Life, 1876–1915*. San Francisco: HarperCollins, 1991.

Schuyler, David. *Village & Farm Cottages*. Watkins Glen, NY: American Life, 1982.

Scott, Frank. *Suburban Home Grounds*. New York: D. Appleton and Co., 1870.

Scott, Frank J., and David Schuyler. *Victorian Gardens: Part I, Suburban Homes*. Watkins Glen, NY: American Life, 1982.

Scott, M. H. Baillie. *Houses and Gardens Arts and Crafts Interiors*. New York: Antique Collectors' Club, 1995.

Seebohm, Caroline, and Christopher Skyes. *Private Landscapes: Creating Form, Vistas, and Mystery in the Garden*. New York: Clarkson N. Potter, 1989.

Skelsey, Alice. *Orchids*. Alexandria, VA: Time-Life Books, 1978.

Stickland, Sue. *Heirloom Vegetables: A Home Gardener's Guide to Finding and Growing Vegetables from the Past*. New York: Simon & Schuster, 1998.

Strong, Roy. *A Celebration of Gardens*. Portland, OR: Timber Press, 1991.

———. *Small Period Gardens: A Practical Guide to Design and Planting*. New York: Rizzoli, 1992.

———. *Successful Small Gardens: New Designs for Time-Conscious Gardeners*. New York: Rizzoli, 1995.

Stuart, David. *The Garden Triumphant: A Victorian Legacy*. New York: Harper & Row, 1988.

Tabor, Grace. *Old-Fashioned Gardening: A History and a Reconstruction*. New York: McBride, Nast and Company, 1913.

Tankard, Judith B. *The Gardens of Ellen Biddle Shipman*. Sagaponack, NY: Sagapress, 1996.

Tankard, Judith B., and Martin A. Wood. *Gertrude Jekyll at Munstead Wood*. Sagaponack, NY: Sagapress, 1996.

Taylor, Albert D., and Gordon D. Cooper. *The Complete Garden*. New York: Garden City Publishing, 1921.

Teyssot, Georges, ed. *The American Lawn*. New York: Princeton Architectural Press, 1999.

Thomas, Graham S. *The Art of Gardening with Roses*. New York: Henry Holt and Company, 1991.

Thomas, John. *The American Fruit Culturist*. New York: William Wood and Company, 1867.

Thompson, Robert. *Gardener's Assistant*. 2 vols. London: The Gresham Publishing Company, 1909.

Thompson, Sylvia. *The Kitchen Garden.* New York: Bantam Books, 1995.

Thorpe, Patricia. *The American Weekend Gardener.* New York: Random House, 1988.

Tice, Patricia M. *Gardening in America, 1830–1910.* Rochester, NY: Strong Museum, 1984.

Toogood, Alan. *The Sheltered Garden.* North Pomfret, VT: Trafalgar Square Publishing, 1989.

Tooley, Michael, and Primrose Amander. *Gertrude Jekyll: Essays on the Life of a Working Amateur.* Durham, UK: Michaelmas Books, 1995.

Vaughan's Seed Store Chicago Illustrated Catalog. Chicago: Vaughan, 1891, 1896.

Verey, Rosemary. *Classic Garden Design: How to Adapt and Re-create Garden Features of the Past.* New York: Random House, 1989.

Vick's Illustrated Catalogue and Floral Guide. Rochester, NY: James Vick, 1865–1885.

Vick's Illustrated Monthly Magazine. Rochester, NY: James Vick, 1878–1888.

Wallinger, Rosamund. *Gertrude Jekyll's Lost Garden: The Restoration of an Edwardian Masterpiece.* Suffolk, UK: Antique Collector's Club, 2000.

Waugh, F.A. *Formal Design in Landscape Architecture.* New York: Orange Judd Company, 1927.

Weaver, Lawrence. *Houses and Gardens by E. L. Lutyens.* Suffolk, UK: Antique Collector's Club, 1994.

Weidenmann, Jacob. *Beautifying Country Homes: A Handbook of Landscape Gardening.* New York: Orange Judd Company, 1870.

Whiteside, Katherine, and Mick Hales, photographer. *Classic Bulbs.* New York: Villard Books, 1991.

Williams, Susan. *Savory Suppers and Fashionable Feasts: Dining in Victorian America.* Knoxville, TN: University of Tennessee Press, 1996.

Woodhead, Eileen. *Early Canadian Gardening: An 1827 Nursery Catalogue.* Montreal: McGill-Queen's University Press, 1998.

Wright, Richardson. *The Story of Gardening.* New York: Dodd, Mead and Company, 1934.

Wyman, Donald. *Shrubs & Vines for American Gardens.* New York: Macmillan, 1969.

———. *Trees for American Gardens: Definitive Guide to Identification and Cultivation.* New York: Macmillan, 1990.

———. *Wyman's Gardening Encyclopedia.* New York: Macmillan, 1986.

———. "Plants and Gardens," In *Origins of American Horticulture, A Handbook.* New York: Brooklyn Botanic Gardens, 1967.

———. "Introductory Dates of Familiar Trees, Shrubs and Vines." In *Origins of American Horticulture, A Handbook.* New York: Brooklyn Botanic Garden, 1967.

Yang, Linda. *Plants for Problem Places: How to Turn Any Difficult Site into a Beautiful Easy-Care Garden.* Boston: Houghton Mifflin Company, 1997.

———. *Taylor's Weekend Gardening Guide to Topiaries and Espaliers: Plus Other Designs for Shaping Plants.* Boston: Houghton Mifflin Company, 1999.

Yepsen, Roger. *A Celebration of Heirloom Vegetables: Growing and Cooking Old-Time Varieties.* New York: Workman Publishing Company, 1998.

Yoch, James J. *Landscaping the American Dream: The Gardens and Film Sets of Florence Yoch.* New York: Abrams, 1989.

PHOTO CREDITS

INDEX